Connecting Boys with Books

What Libraries Can Do

Michael Sullivan

American Library Association
Chicago   2003

While extensive effort has gone into ensuring the reliability of information appearing in this book, the publisher makes no warranty, express or implied, on the accuracy or reliability of the information, and does not assume and hereby disclaims any liability to any person for any loss or damage caused by errors or omissions in this publication.

Composition and design by ALA Editions in Aperto and Berkeley using QuarkXPress 5.0 for the PC

Printed on 50-pound white offset, a pH-neutral stock, and bound in 10-point coated cover stock by Victor Graphics

The paper used in this publication meets the minimum requirements of American National Standard for Information Sciences—Permanence of Paper for Printed Library Materials, ANSI Z39.48-1992.∞

Library of Congress Cataloging-in-Publication Data

Sullivan, Michael, 1967 Aug. 30-
    Connecting boys with books : what libraries can do / by Michael Sullivan.
       p. cm.
    Includes bibliographical references and index.
    ISBN 0-8389-0849-7 (alk. paper)
    1. Children's libraries—Activity programs. 2. Young adults' libraries—Activity programs. 3. Boys—Books and reading. 4. Reading promotion. 5. Reading—Sex differences. I. Title.
Z718.1.S85 2003
028.5'5—dc21   2003006962

Printed in the United States of America

07 06 05 04 03   5 4 3 2 1

To Helen Marie Sullivan,
who always wanted me
to be a reader and a writer

CONTENTS

ACKNOWLEDGMENTS   *vii*

FOREWORD   *ix*

INTRODUCTION   *xi*

Chapter 1   Lost Boys   *1*

Chapter 2   Reaching Out to Boys and Men   *8*

Chapter 3   It's Still about Books   *22*

Chapter 4   From Story Hour to Independent Reading   *44*

Chapter 5   Chess, Games, and Challenges   *57*

Chapter 6   The Power of Stories   *73*

Chapter 7   Reading, Talking, and Promoting Books   *95*

CONCLUSION   *109*

BIBLIOGRAPHY   *113*

INDEX   *117*

ACKNOWLEDGMENTS

Citations never seem to tell the story of where a book comes from, and in the making of this book there are many people who have had their part. First I want to thank the dedicated librarians with whom I have had the privilege of working, who have shared their ideas, their interests, and their enthusiasm with me, and many of whom freely gave their input on this book itself. Foremost among them are Phyllis Danko, Mindy Hawkins, Lesley Gaudreau, Susan MacDonald, Ellen Tirone, and Stacy Debole.

Other librarians have shared their programming ideas and experience when I truly needed personal insights. Prominent among these is Donna Beales. Professor Margaret Bush has had an enormous impact on this work, and on me, as she has had on so many of the children's specialists in the field today.

Renée Vaillencourt McGrath at ALA Editions has been a constant encouragement in my writing, and it is thanks to her that the opportunity to write this book arose.

And finally, of course, are the fine young men for whom so many of these programs were offered: Derek, Zack, Carmine, Joey, Steven, Alex, Chris, Ben, A. J., Matthew, Sky, Peter, Kris, David, and all the rest. You carry a heavy burden, to prove that the men of the coming age can be decent, smart, and just one step better than the generation, my generation, that has come before. I have enjoyed every minute working with you, teaching you, reading to you, playing against you in chess, and watching you grow up. I hope to see you pave the way for a generation yet to come.

FOREWORD
by Jon Scieszka

You probably don't need Michael Sullivan to tell you that many of our boys are having trouble with reading. The U.S. Department of Education statistics show boys an average of one and a half grades behind girls in reading. Seventy percent of kids in remedial classes are boys. Boys are not the majority showing up for library programs. Boys are the majority saying they spend no time reading for pleasure.

But we do need Michael Sullivan to challenge us to change these statistics, and tell us in practical and concrete terms what libraries can do to connect boys with books. Thank goodness he has.

If you care at all about kids and reading—read this book. If you don't care about kids and reading—read this book. In fact, you probably shouldn't even bother to read the rest of the foreword. Just go ahead and read this book.

If you are still here, I guess I can explain that Sullivan does a marvelous job of illuminating some of the factors that affect boys and reading. He describes the differences in boys' and girls' learning styles. He examines the lack of male reading role models. He offers a slew of ideas for effective programming for boys, a cornucopia of book lists for boys. He takes a clear-eyed look at the profession of being a librarian and invokes the ethical imperative of the ALA Bill of Rights to provide "equal service to all."

I can't believe you are still out here in the front of the book reading this. Librarians have a unique opportunity to connect boys with books in a way that inspires them. Libraries can offer boys the choice and immediate

---

Jon Scieszka is the author of *The Stinky Cheese Man*, the Time Warp Trio series, and plenty of other books he has tried to connect with kids. He is also the founder of a literacy program for boys called "Guys Read" at www.guysread.com.

engagement that they prefer in reading. Libraries can be a safe and nurturing place in those dangerous hours when most kids get in trouble after school. Librarians can be the ones to change the problem we know many of our boys are having with reading.

Now turn the page, and let's start changing the world.

INTRODUCTION

I remember, I remember,
The fir trees dark and high;
I used to think their slender tops
Were close against the sky:
It was a childish ignorance,
But now 'tis little joy
To know I'm farther off from heav'n
Than when I was a boy.

—Thomas Hood, "I Remember" [1]

This is a book for all those who sincerely believe that library services and reading are too good to be missed. It is for people who believe, as I do, that good reading habits are essential to getting the most out of life, and that those habits are difficult or impossible to acquire if they are not learned early. It focuses specifically on boys in that period when they are no longer children but not yet teenagers, from eight to twelve years old, what we know as the "tween" years. This book is both a warning and a celebration of the things that make boys different from girls and the things that make this age so different from others. I have come to believe that both the concern and the exaltation are necessary if we are to open up to boys the great expanse of possibilities that a healthy reading life can provide.

In developing a book about library services for boys, I wanted to avoid any hint of misogyny. It is difficult for men to talk about gender and not sound discriminatory, especially when the topic is the special needs of boys. That may be why so little has been made of this issue in public debate. There are plenty of children's librarians and elementary educators who are concerned about choosing books for boys; designing services for boys is a more delicate matter. But the issues here have nothing to do with disparaging the needs of girls or the ability of women to serve boys. It is not a matter of separating the sexes, and I will not be talking about men and boys painting themselves in war colors and pounding on drums in the woods. I will be looking at ways to make the things we do for everybody more welcoming for boys.

Indeed, gender separation could have a negative effect on the development of boys. One of our goals when working with boys should be to counter the flat, stereotypical view of masculinity that prevails in today's media, and mixed-gender groupings in early adolescence can help. As Angela Phillips points out in *The Trouble with Boys*, "Where adolescents socialize in mixed groups there will be far less pressure on boys to conform to male behavioral norms. . . . If girls are part of a boy's peer group he is far less likely to treat them as objects to be leered at, or sneered at, and he will almost certainly find that these friendships open up the closed doors of the place in which he stowed his feelings."[2]

I would add a contextual note. Boys and girls mixing together in a supportive, positive, and productive environment is more likely to mute behavioral norms. Today, we see mixed-gender groupings in "hangout" situations, and we know that peer pressure is affecting younger and younger kids. It is clear that eleven- and twelve-year-olds may be acting out the same power relationship scenarios that fourteen- and fifteen-year-olds were exhibiting in a previous generation: flirt and impress, intimidate and dominate. This is where the library comes into the picture.

The problem is that the gatherings in America's libraries are not truly integrated. The presence of boys in libraries is rare. It is much more usual to see all elementary-aged girls in the library or at a library program than it is to see all elementary-aged boys. If we believe that providing opportunities to experience mixed-gender situations in positive, creative settings is the best way to socialize children, then being more inviting to boys will actually benefit girls as well.

This book is offered largely in response to a simple fact that almost all children's librarians, school librarians, and elementary school teachers, indeed all who work in childhood education, know deep within their bones: boys do not read as much as girls. This is in the face of the general belief that children in general read less than they should. Even in this modern, high-tech world, reading is vital in developing verbal skills and higher-level thinking. Culturally, reading promises to promote a more socially beneficial view of masculinity than the stereotypical messages of today's media.

One of the most effective tools that libraries use to promote reading is programming. Programs bring people from our communities into our libraries for enrichment, enlightenment, and entertainment, and they tie these activities to the collections we have built. Given this traditional role, it is imperative that librarians design programming with an eye toward serving the needs of boys. Effective programming can foster good reading habits for boys, and give boys a real life lesson in community.

There are great challenges to programming for boys; otherwise everyone would be doing it. We cannot overcome these challenges by simply booking a speaker to talk on a topic near and dear to most boys' hearts. We must apply all the aspects of programming, from public relations, to content, to follow-up and outreach, to address the problem. In many cases, this will mean rethinking our approach and maybe doing a little soul-searching as to how we really feel about our work and our audience.

The following pages will lay out the challenges as they exist today, the ground being lost as boys fall behind in reading, especially during preadolescence. It will acknowledge the difficulties that boys face in becoming readers: cultural factors that discourage boys from reading, stereotypes that keep boys away from libraries, the lack of male role models in schools and libraries, and the absence of fathers in the library experience. These challenges can leave boys with an impression of libraries as an entirely female realm.

Few men perform children's library services. If more did, then more boys might identify reading with masculinity. Though we should work to resolve this discrepancy, male librarians are not necessary in order to serve boys. Women who work with boys should realize the difference between the reading habits of boys and girls and consider carefully the things they can do to help both. Still, it is vital that men take an active role in libraries, to model good reading habits and dispel the myths of manhood that discourage boys from becoming lifelong readers. Also, collections need to be altered to reflect the interests of boys. We need to go beyond a few picture books about trucks and a skateboarder biography to provide real recreational and informational reading.

What kinds of programs appeal to boys? There are programs that help boys keep the love of a good story as they face the uncertainties of the early elementary years. As boys develop a greater sense of the difference between the genders, they face a gap between the adults they see and the men they are to become. This is when so many boys lose the connection of reading as a pleasurable experience in itself, rather than a utilitarian exercise.

Boys will respond to programs that feed their competitive spirit. Should we relegate competition to the athletic fields? All the benefits of healthy competition can be had in a setting that emphasizes the development of the mind. Challenge the minds of boys and they will be more inclined to exercise them. Reward boys for using their minds and they will learn to respect intellectual accomplishments.

Programs that give boys an avenue of expression will feed their confidence and self-image, giving them positive ways of establishing a reason for pride. Programs that model reading for pleasure and allow boys to hear stories read out loud will give them confidence in their own reading. Promoting books that speak to boys will feed their excitement to strike out and explore reading independently.

Inherent in this work is the belief that reading is necessary in order to develop a young person into a freethinking, productive member of our democratic modern society. Equally important, building a community of readers is the best way to promote reading to young people, and libraries with their programming play a vital role in creating that community. Libraries can bring fathers, sons, and male role models into the library and promote a collection that serves the growing minds of boys. Effective programming that recognizes boys' interests, learning styles, and needs will help bring boys and books together and turn interested participants into avid readers.

NOTES

1. *Oxford Dictionary of Quotations* (London: Oxford Univ. Pr., 1955), 253.
2. Angela Phillips, *The Trouble with Boys* (New York: Basic Books, 1994), 256.

Chapter 1

Lost Boys

God bless all little boys who look like Puck,
With wide eyes, wider mouths and stickout ears,
Rash little boys who stay alive by luck
And heaven's favour in this world of tears.

—Arthur Guiterman, *"Blessing on Little Boys"*[1]

It should not come as a shock that boys fall far behind girls in reading, especially in the middle elementary years. Boys read less and do less recreational reading than girls do. The scholarship on this point is clear.

The National Assessment of Educational Progress (NAEP) reported that not only do fourth-grade girls score higher in reading than boys, but the gap increased between 1998 and 2000.[2] The United States Department of Education statistics show that boys are an average of one and a half grades behind girls in reading.[3] Boys are two to three times more likely than girls to be diagnosed with a reading disability, depending on different definitions and methods of diagnosis.[4]

The gap does not seem to disappear as children age. The 1996 NAEP report showed seventeen-year-old girls an average of fourteen points ahead of boys in reading on a five-hundred-point scale.[5] UCLA freshmen are asked each year how many hours they spend reading for pleasure. In 1998, 35 percent of males answered "none" as opposed to 22 percent of females.[6] Frankly, both numbers are frightening.

1

It will also be no surprise that boys suffer from educational and social ills at a much greater rate than girls do. In 1994, 85 percent of special education students in America were male.[7] Seventy percent of children in remedial classes are male.[8] Boys commit suicide at a rate four times higher than girls and are diagnosed as mentally disturbed four times as often.[9] In 1996 there were 1.7 million more women than men enrolled in college in the U.S.[10] The situation is worse where other factors such as race, class, and economics add to disadvantages of gender. A 1992 study found that twice as many black girls were graduating from college as compared to black boys.[11]

None of this seems surprising to many in the field of children's education. It would be stunning to see a major study prove that boys read more than girls. It would be shocking to see more girls in jail or failing in school. However, are these trends merely coincidental, an aberration against probability? Worse still, are they unavoidable, a mere fact of existence that boys cannot change? Librarians, whether they are school media specialists, school library administrators, public library children's librarians, or public library administrators, have to believe they are not. A lack of reading may not cause these problems for boys, but an active interest in reading is sure to be a part of the solution.

FRUSTRATED COMMUNICATORS

Better build schoolrooms for "the boy"
Than cells and gibbets for "the man"
—Eliza Cook,
"A Song for the Ragged Schools"[12]

You have probably heard the arguments. Boys, whether through nature or nurture, are less able to express feelings, are more likely to put on a tough façade and act aggressively when confused or frightened. Boys who feel it is unmanly to cry, who are unsure of the response they will get to a plea for empathy, and who have not developed higher forms of creative expression are left with aggression as the only acceptable form of self-expression at their disposal. It is a frustrating position to be in, not being able to communicate. Those of us who see the fits of anger in a toddler who knows how to speak but does not know the words to make herself understood are very aware of the power of that frustration. However, we do not always see the frustration in a nine-year-old acting out, or the antisocial behavior of a fourteen-year-old. While both two-year-old boys and two-year-old girls throw temper tantrums, usually the boys are showing that frustration in later years.

Nature versus Nurture

Why do the boys have so few communication tools? Partly, it is because boys learn differently than girls, and that means they read differently as well. Freudians have often reduced the difference to inborn drives—for boys to master their world, for girls to understand their world. Boys look to separate and gain perspective, believing their world to be made up of objects that have uses and rules that must be understood. Meanwhile, girls seek engagement to understand human relations, believing the world to be shaped by personal interaction. Hence boys read for information; girls read for methods of communication and cooperation.[13]

Boys appear to be more dependent on structure in their learning styles. They work toward goals and outcomes, building pieces into a whole. The old adage about boys being better in math and girls in language skills seems to have passed the test of time. Math is concrete and conceptual; language is fluid and intricate. Boys can get a math problem "right"; it is very difficult to read a book "right." Some British schools are trying to address boys' reading troubles with a special period of structured learning about reading skills separate from regular reading instruction, emphasizing building-block concepts to raise the confidence of students, particularly boys.[14]

Behaviorists will argue that these are learned behaviors or differences, introduced into children's psyches from the moment a blue or a pink knit hat is placed on a child's head in the hospital nursery. For the librarian who seeks to serve children, especially boys, in the vital middle- to upper-elementary years, the cause is immaterial. Both sides agree that, largely, this is how children end up acting. Add to this the fact that boys live in a world where women play the most visible role by far, and a boy is left with a drive to act, to control his world, and few examples of someone like him (a man) doing just that. Already frustrated by a lack of direction, he now sees a world where apparently only women do anything productive, and he starts to feel that he has no place. Unable to articulate such a subtle feeling at such a tender age, he turns to simple and direct communication, in both words and actions, and is disciplined for "acting out."

BOYS, MEN, AND SUPERMEN

Some have argued that this is why boys latch onto superheroes. Give a mus-cle-bound hero a cape, a mask, and a catchy nickname and you have all the things that an increasingly alienated boy needs to envision a place for him-self in society. Superheroes are usually male, they are unquestionably good, and they have a purpose in life, which they can serve through fighting (dom-inating others) and protecting those less powerful than themselves (thereby asserting their own powerfulness). They get all this without ambiguity, fear of accountability, or the need to depend on others.[15]

As boys age, they find that television and movies, restrained in the length and scope of their messages, feed audiences this same kind of unambiguous world view. A character that you will know for less than two hours cannot have many layers. An act of violence on screen cannot have long-term conse-quences because there is no long term. Problems are most likely to be solved by force because force is something that can be portrayed visually, where thought cannot. Our media tell boys to grow up to be strong, aggressive, vio-lent, and unheeding of consequences. The mind, they tell them, is at best irrelevant, and at worst distracting. When boys act on these instructions, we call them dumb, refuse to hire them, or put them in jail.

Angela Phillips, noted feminist and author of *The Trouble with Boys*, points out that, "Hard men do not make themselves. Lessons in violence, indifference, and separation are provided every day for every male child. Learning them is a part of learning to survive as a boy, and unlearning them is a great deal to expect of anyone. . . ."[16]

The Remedy Is Reading

Do we abandon boys to this flat, stereotyped vision of what a man should be? No, we encourage boys to read instead. Reading develops the power of lan-guage and higher-level thought, giving younger boys the tools to envision their place in society and to express themselves in a satisfying manner. For older boys, reading and the community spirit embodied in an active library can provide more nuances to the picture, with more promise for development in this complex, modern world. A character in a book has time to work through problems and experience the consequences of his actions. He can have a place in society and do things that benefit others without those others having to be in dire circumstances. Beyond the psychological advantages, reading can give boys the skills to be productive and to avoid the frustration of the intellectually powerless in an information age.

THE IMPORTANCE OF PROGRAMMING

Girls read more than boys, so it seems axiomatic that girls will be a greater presence in libraries. Library programs, though usually not gender-specific, draw more girls than boys. Since the vast majority of children's librarians are female, it can be expected that they will understand and respond to the needs of girls more easily then they will to those of boys. It is reasonable to say that girls attend more programs because they read more and so they are simply "there." It is also reasonable to assume that libraries tilt their programs more toward girls in more or less subtle ways because they are the more receptive audience.

It's 3:00 P.M. Do You Know Where Your Son Is?

Gender-biased programming is a potentially devastating blow to boys, given the recent insights into destructive and self-destructive behavior of youths during unsupervised time. That destructive behavior is most prevalent during after-school hours when many library programs occur. A 1993 study in the journal *Pediatrics* outlines a host of ill effects associated directly with a lack of adult supervision in the hours after school: substance abuse, risk taking, depression, and failing grades. Parental supervision, the study suggests, is best, but active engagement is also beneficial. "Those who 'hang out,'" the study concludes, "are most likely to engage in problem behavior."[17] A Carnegie Corporation study in 1992 linked unsupervised after-school time with higher high school dropout rates and gang involvement.[18]

A more recent study reaffirmed all these ill effects and added a few more ominous ones. It showed that after-school hours are the peak time for juvenile crime and the time when juveniles are most likely to be the victims of violence. It is also the time when teens are most likely to experiment with sex or to try explicitly violent video games. Lack of supervision is the common factor, and the study showed that one in three American children between the ages of ten and twelve are unsupervised in the after-school hours.

On the positive side, in study after study, after-school programs proved to significantly decrease the negative behaviors of at-risk youth.[19] This became clear to me one evening when I experienced one of the most dreaded visits. The police showed up at my library looking for a boy who never made it home from school, expecting to ask the kids in the library if anyone had seen him. As it turned out, the missing boy was there in the library, where his parents would never have expected him. He had been playing chess all afternoon and lost track of time.

An Ethical Imperative

Girls read more than boys do; girls are in the library more; libraries develop programs to fit their audience. These realities and this reasoning do not show sufficient respect for the calamitous future that awaits boys who grow up as nonreaders. They also abandon boys to the social ills that libraries can alleviate by effective programming for youth. Article V of the American Library Association's Library Bill of Rights mandates that "library services, materials, and programs be available to all members of the community the library serves, without regard to gender. . . ."[20] The ethics of our profession demand that we give equal service. The principles that underpin our profession tell us to instill in our customers a love of reading and to place that as one of our top service objectives. So let's get serious about library services for boys.

NOTES

1. *Pocket Book of Quotations* (New York: Pocket Books, 1952), 20.
2. Lucille Renwick, "What's the Buzz?" *Instructor* 111 (August 2001): 8.
3. Christina Hoff Sommers, *The War against Boys* (New York: Simon & Schuster, 2000), 14.
4. Slavica K. Katusic, Robert C. Colligan, William J. Barbaresi, et al., "Incidence of Reading Disability in a Population-Based Birth Cohort, 1976–1982, Rochester, Minn.," *Mayo Clinic Proceedings* 76 (2001): 1081.
5. Sommers, *The War against Boys,* 33.
6. Ibid., 164.
7. Angela Phillips, *The Trouble with Boys* (New York: Basic Books, 1994), 19.
8. Stan Steiner, "Where Have All the Men Gone?: Male Role Models in the Reading Crisis," *PNLA Quarterly* 64 (summer 2000): 17.
9. Michael Cart, "What about Boys?" *Booklist* 96 (January 1, 2000 & January 15, 2000): 892.
10. Sommers, *The War against Boys,* 30.
11. Phillips, *The Trouble with Boys,* 18.
12. *Oxford Dictionary of Quotations* (London: Oxford Univ. Pr., 1955), 156.
13. Deborah Langerman, "Books and Boys: Gender Preferences and Book Selection," *School Library Journal* 36 (March 1990): 132–36.
14. Sommers, *The War against Boys,* 167–68.
15. Phillips, *The Trouble with Boys,* 43–44.
16. Ibid., 33.
17. Jean L. Richardson, Barbara Radziszewska, Clyde W. Dent, et al., "Relationship between After-School Care of Adolescents and Substance Use, Risk Taking, Depressed Mood, and Academic Achievement," *Pediatrics* 92 (July 1993): 36.

18. Peter Witt and Dwayne Baker, "Developing After-School Programs for Youth in High-Risk Environments," *Journal of Physical Education, Recreation & Dance* 69 (November/December 1997): 18.
19. Sandford A. Newmann, James Alan Fox, Edward A. Flynn, et al., *America's After-School Choice: The Prime Time for Juvenile Crime, or Youth Enrichment and Achievement* (Washington, D.C.: Fight Crime: Invest in Kids, 2000), 18.
20. Access to Library Resources and Services regardless of Gender or Sexual Orientation, 2000, available at http://www.ala.org/alaorg/oif/acc_gend.html/. Accessed July 22, 2002.

Chapter 2

Reaching Out
to Boys and Men

"Why don't you go and do something?" my mother would say.
"I am doing something. I'm reading."
"It isn't healthy just lying there with your nose in a book,"
she would say, just as she said to my father.

—Robert MacNeil, *Reader's Quotation Book*[1]

Certainly, the number of librarians who consciously discourage boys from using the library just because they are boys is very small, but they do exist. The only real antidote to such people is vigilance among the responsible members of the profession. We must police our own and pressure such people to mend their ways or find a more suitable profession. These people are not the heart of the problem.

AN ABSENCE OF MEN

The real struggle must be against a lack of focus on the needs of boys. We must counteract a vision of problems and possible solutions blurred by misunderstanding, past practices, and wide gaps of experience. One major contributing factor to this blurring is the absence of men in children's libraries.

It was at a conference of children's librarians that it first hit me just how rare men are in the field. At the first break in the program I headed for the restrooms, only to find the sign on the men's room door covered up by a piece of white notebook paper on which was hastily scrawled "Women." Working under the assumption that men never came to these conferences, the author of the sign must not have noticed that there was a man in the crowd of nearly two hundred.

In any case, the predominance of women in the field of children's librarianship was clearly highlighted. Women made up 83.4 percent of the profession in the United States in 1998, and the few men in the field experience what sociologist Christine Williams calls the "glass escalator," meaning they are pressured into administrative roles.[2] That leaves few men to do children's work. In more than a decade in the profession, I have actually met only one other active male children's librarian, though I have met a male library director who does children's work and a few male directors who have children's backgrounds. The sum total is miniscule. Men simply do not do children's work in public libraries or in elementary school media centers. When most children think of librarians, they think of women.

The reasons for this discrepancy are many, and they need to be addressed, though not in this forum. Suffice it to say that the lack of men contributes to the perception of the feminine library, and that does a disservice to boys. Librarians face two challenges in this regard—first, to find a way to be understanding and inclusive of boys, even when most of us have no firsthand knowledge of being a boy; and second, to dispel the perception that libraries are a female realm, so that boys will take the opportunity to see how welcoming we are. All our efforts at being welcoming to boys will go for naught if we fail to get past this most basic belief.

A BOY'S PERSPECTIVE

But fidgety Phil,
He won't sit still;
He wriggles
And giggles,
And then I declare,
Swings backwards and forwards,
And tilts up his chair.

—Heinrich Hoffman, *"Fidgety Philip"*[3]

So how do you relate to a boy if you never were one? First, see the situation from the boy's point of view. Even with all the advances toward equal employment and equal responsibility in the home, the fact of the matter remains that mothers tend to spend a great deal more time performing child care than fathers do. Child care providers who enter the home are more likely to be female, and parents who are absent from the family are more likely to be male. Add that to the fact that most elementary teachers, school librarians, and children's librarians are female, and the boy staring up at you with a guilty grin is likely to be seeing a world largely devoid of men.

Boys know the difference between men and women, and they know they are destined to become men. Unfortunately, life gives boys very few clues as to what that means. Girls see a great deal of adult women, and though they may get a narrow view of the possibilities that are open to them, they at least see a world where they have a place. Boys see a world where their place will be "out," somewhere they do not understand and cannot picture. We tell girls over and over that they do not have to fit into the stereotypical roles they see around them; they can do anything a man can do. Yet boys often see no roles for themselves in the future at all, and this leads to frustration. Boys grow up with the sneaking suspicion that they just do not belong.

Squeezing Boys Out

With men largely absent from their lives, boys rely upon direct verbal clues from their mothers and female caregivers to help them shape their own views of what it is to be male.[4] If the women in their lives reinforce the idea that they have no role "here," then boys will continue to think their place is some-where "out there," which is not a welcoming or comforting idea.

Boys tend to be more loud, boisterous, and physical than girls. When they exhibit these traits in the library, they are shushed, glared at, and made to feel unwelcome in a hundred different ways—that is, if they are not actu-ally told to leave. We can say that this type of behavior is inappropriate in libraries, but then we might as well admit that the boys are right, they do not belong here. We cannot define one-half of our population out of our libraries and still claim to be open and inclusive. It is far better to serve a range of needs by defining space and times for certain types of activity than it is to serve some narrow picture of proper library behavior.

In truth, we already do this. We define an hour some morning as story time in one part of the children's room, and we do things such as group singing that we might frown upon at other times and in other areas of the library. We make a sticky mess with glue and markers and think nothing of wiping down the tables after the kids leave. But when four boys gather around a table for a game of paper football after school, we tell them not to talk so loud and say things like, "By the way, I don't ever want to see scraps of paper on the floor again." In my experience, the loudest people in most libraries are not the school-age boys, but the elderly people whose hearing is failing, followed closely by the library staff themselves. We just define gossip behind the desk and in the large-print section as appropriate.

In urban public libraries, where concentrations are high and nerves become frayed, boys are especially likely to be squeezed out. We need to ask ourselves how much we are willing to give up for a library that is both neat as a pin and pin-drop quiet. In Everett, Massachusetts, one of the most congested parts of the metropolitan Boston area, our people counters indicated that on an average day more than one hundred customers came through our children's area door in the hour after school ended, and countless more entered through the adult area and came downstairs. On a busy day, we could double that. The vast majority of these people were elementary and middle school students, there because nobody was at home to be with them. An economically challenged and racially diverse community, the city of Everett consisted of households that were either single parent or had both parents working.

MAKING BOYS WELCOME

The first half hour of the onrush was bedlam as groups came and went, claimed their tables, unpacked their book bags, caught up with friends, and stretched out after a day of sitting at desks. None of this, of course, was allowed upstairs in the adult reading room because adults deserve their space as well. At three o'clock we would settle the groups down and start the afternoon programs. We left one area with tables and chairs where kids could talk, eat, and relax, while the rest of the children's room became a place for reading and quiet study. The important point is that normal kid behavior, even normal boy behavior, was not wrong or banned; it always had a place and time.

Many libraries have designated quiet study areas but have no place set aside for social interaction and relaxation for kids, and very few libraries provide a transitional time where rules are relaxed to allow kids to be kids. You can use that time to interact with a population that does not fit your profile of the standard library user. Stand at the door one day greeting every kid with a slip of paper. Ask them to write down their favorite joke, and after a few minutes stand up on a chair and read some of them aloud. Show kids that what is natural and fun to them is welcome, and they will be more likely to tailor their activities to the appropriate time and place.

The same principle applies to food. Many libraries still ban food. (Staff members, of course, have a place to eat and make coffee, and many of them drink coffee at their desks or in their offices.) Telling an eleven-year-old boy not to eat, especially in the mid-afternoon, can be the equivalent of telling a stream to run uphill. Then, when library staff find candy wrappers stuffed behind bookshelves they say, "See, this is why we have a no food rule." Mark an area where food is allowed, a place where noise and conduct rules are loose. Then the candy wrappers will end up in the trashcans, and growing boys will not think you are singling them out for torture.

Giving Boys a Role

While we denounce boys for being unproductive and disruptive on the one hand, on the other hand we deny them a more constructive and productive role. We do this by absenting them from responsibility. Remember, boys are more likely to see women with responsibility for others' needs than they are to see men with such responsibility. The fact that men have responsibilities outside of the home and school is irrelevant; boys do not see it, so it does not exist. We recognize a parallel problem among girls who do not see that women have a role outside of the home, and we address it with Take Your Daughter to Work Day.

Boys have little firsthand knowledge of men caring for others. Even as they grow old enough to know intellectually that dad works, or that men have responsibilities too, preadolescent boys will not internalize this easily. While they may have a set of chores they are responsible for in the home, they may still be unsure what, in general, the world expects of them. They know what women do, but what do men do?

Teachers and librarians used to ask girls to clean up, to set up, or to provide other helpful services while the boys were left to fend for themselves, already occupied by high-energy play. This was a matter of course. We are probably beyond this now, but even if we ask boys and girls to help equally, we need to realize that girls are modeled responsible behavior because they can identify with adults who are like them. Too often, boys have no such models. They may desperately need to feel useful, but they are too unsure of their place to act on that need.

As boys get older and begin to interact more independently from adults, their play becomes more physical and their surroundings become more chaotic. This does not sit well with many librarians, whose lives are tied up with creating order out of chaos. Many libraries have rules against rearranging furniture, playing games, or even lying on the floor. (More about games later.) When librarians see these things going on, the boys are usually in the center of things, and the first reaction is often, "Clean that up!" or even "Get out!" We need to let boys be boys sometimes, and focus instead on a lesson in responsibility. Let them move the furniture, crash out on the floor, and tear pieces of paper into tiny strips if that is what they want, as long as they return everything to normal before they go.

Girls, more confident in their place, are likely to finish tasks, while boys will stand by or, more likely, act out their frustration in distracting or counterproductive behavior. After all, if it is the girls' role to clean up a mess, what does that leave boys to do? It is up to us as educators and caregivers to reinforce the responsibility of all to contribute, to insist that boys do their part. Some will jump at the chance with little encouragement, but some will be unsure of their place and react accordingly—that is, like children at play. Angela Phillips characterizes the latter group's behavior as insecurity based on a lack of gender identification.[5] These are the boys who will benefit most from a firm affirmation that they do have a role. Battle their insecurity not by red-penciling their natural tendencies, but by reinforcing a need to be responsible to others. It is not quite being a superhero, but being responsible for their library and the people who are in it will make boys feel more like men.

Enforcing a standard of behavior that requires quiet, rule-bound activity without any physical component is inherently prejudicial against boys. On the other hand, advocates of "girl power" maintain that allowing boys to engage in unchecked rough play while girls do task work reinforces limited roles for girls. These two trends combined teach girls a narrow sense of place and allow boys to continue without any sense of place at all. It is best for all that both of these practices fade away.

Group Work

Working in groups is one way to foster cooperation. Girls enjoy working together, while boys prefer to work alone. But both girls and boys gravitate toward helping parents of the same gender. The child initiates contact based on identification with the parent and a desire to socialize with him or her. The outcome, though, is a lesson in responsibility: if we work together, then my success depends partly on you. For boys, a little group work can go a long way toward encouraging responsibility.

This one-on-one accountability is a first step toward community. However, since caregivers are most often female, girls experience this much more often than boys do. That's why girls are more comfortable in group work settings. If boys do not experience this type of accountability, they will be less likely to work effectively with others in later years. They may gravitate toward the first communal setting in which they feel comfortable and accepted, the purpose of which may be destructive rather than constructive. We have all seen adolescent and preadolescent boys go that route.

For a man working with children, this is easy. Boys will gravitate toward cooperative efforts with a man, and in my experience it is always a boy who asks to be my partner in teamwork activities. Women who work with children will have to be aware of the different levels of opportunity that boys and girls experience and may have to make a point of initiating cooperative efforts with boys. Debbie Abilock, in a summation of studies looking specifically at the needs of girls in the classroom and the library, took the opportunity to point out that both boys and girls need to be addressed in their weakness, rather than simply letting them lean on their strengths. If boys prefer to take risks and go it alone, and girls prefer to work cooperatively within clearly defined rule structures, then librarians should encourage risk taking in girls and approach boys "with offers of assistance even if they don't request it."[6]

Far from being turned off by such an approach, many boys will be relieved, and even those who hold back will get the message that the library is a place where they can work cooperatively, where they belong. At the very least, we should see that boys do work together with other children of either gender, even when they are wary of it and prefer to work alone. Their reluctance may be nothing more than a lack of experience, and that state may continue through high school if it is not addressed.

Boys enjoy challenge. In our effort to see every child succeed, we sometimes forget to leave room for failure, or we intentionally design the possibility of failure out of our activities. The problem is there is no sense of challenge if you always win. An episode of the television show *The Simpsons* had the prototypical boy character, Bart, placed in a remedial class (and these classes, we know, are predominantly male). The class is playing musical chairs, but there are always enough chairs for everyone to sit in. "Everybody wins!" the teacher exclaims. Bart just groans. What is meant to be comforting is often just boring to the majority of boys.

Challenging Boys

Treat failure lightly, as a step toward real success. Ask children to predict outcomes they have no reason to know, and watch the boys leap at the chance to prognosticate. When experience proves them wrong, you have a very teachable moment in which to express to everyone that trying is part of achieving, and that failing is a part of trying. My favorite line at these moments is about baseball (yes, let's start with the sports analogies early). The best baseball players hit for averages around .300; that means even the all-stars only get it right one out of every three tries. In one commercial, basketball legend Michael Jordan voices over clips of himself missing shot after shot, saying that he missed so many shots because he was always there when the game was on the line. He failed often, but that was why he succeeded.

Boys fear failure less than they fear looking silly. Let them know that taking a shot and falling short is an acceptable part of learning and growth, and they will be more comfortable taking the next shot. In our efforts to encourage risk taking in girls, who tend to internalize feelings of failure and react less strongly to the externalized feeling of embarrassment, we have gone to finding the positive aspect of every attempt. Through a "partial credit" approach to working with children, we have, in effect, programmed failure out of the equation. For boys, who are already more likely to be risk takers, that leaves one burning and frustrating question: "Am I right?" Whatever the answer, boys are more interested in knowing. In years of teaching, coaching, and programming for children, I have been struck over and over at how reluctant many women educators can be to chuckle, shake their heads, and say, "No, that's not it, let's try again."

Remember to include boys when assigning responsibility; encourage cooperative work with boys; challenge boys and help them see failure as part of the road to success, and boys will see you as a welcoming partner, even if you are a "girl." Now, once we are sure that we are welcoming to boys, we need to find a way to get them through the doors in order to experience this openness, but the belief that libraries are not places for boys may still stymie us. Here, a few good role models can go a long way.

BRINGING MEN INTO THE LIBRARY

"So which one is yours?" A dad from the other team was watching my twelve-and-under girls' softball team warming up and started up a conversation in the time-honored way.

"None of them are mine," I answered.

"Yours already through the system?"

"No, I don't have any kids," I replied casually. His reaction was amused, restrained, about as even-keeled as I ever see in this all-too-familiar scenario. I was the only coach in the town softball league who did not have a daughter somewhere in the system, and this tended to surprise people. It is a mark of how proprietary our system of child care and child development has become. So much for needing a village to raise a child. I've always felt that if you accept two seemingly unassailable truths—that kids do not get enough adult attention these days and parents are stretched too thin—then the solution from a societal point of view is clear. People without children need to be involved with kids.

You can make a similar argument when it comes to a male presence in the library. If boys need role models to see that libraries are places for men, and there are not enough men doing children's work in libraries, then we need to bring in nonlibrarians to fill the gap. I don't mean to denigrate the ability of women to serve boys. The reality of service is well within their grasp. It is the perception of the exclusively female library that needs to be overcome so that women who work with children get a chance to reach boys. We think nothing of inviting celebrity athletes to do promotions for libraries, or bringing in authors to model their success. These people are little more than window dressing, a blatant attempt to plant associations in our clients' minds. Why not do the same with men?

Safety Issues

Actually, there are some pragmatic concerns when men work with children. The foremost is safety. Sexual abuse of children is a societal disgrace, no matter how rare the cases may be statistically. Those of us who devote our lives to the care and education of children must be on the greatest alert for their welfare. Certainly, the incidence of child abuse in the public arena is rare, but we must face the fact that most abusers are men. One of the reasons our educational system evolved as it has is that society feels safer with its children in the care of women.

The first step toward making men a part of the library community and still protecting children is the basic background check, which is becoming a part of everyday life in public service. Yes, it is troubling to be asked to surrender your privacy, and worse yet to have to ask, but the world is the way it is. You do not want to put yourself in the position one library was in when it hired me. It had no provision in its personnel policy and had to pass a background check requirement at the first trustees meeting after I joined the staff. The implication was clear: we never needed this before, but we need it now. The only thing that had changed in the interim was the hiring of the first male librarian in anyone's memory, who also happened to have a background in children's services.

The fact is that everyone who works with children must attain a higher level of trust, and background checks are a part of gaining that trust in the modern world. That goes for employees and regular volunteers as well. It is just that the inclusion of men into the mix highlights the importance of such measures. It is best to address the policy on its own merits before the policy is used to address a particular individual or gender. There are many arguments for where to draw the line. Do you require background checks on all volunteers? Only those who work a certain number of hours? Only those who work with the public? Or only those who work with children? These are fruitful discussions to have, but if you draw the line at all, those who work directly with children should be the first ones included.

I have included a boilerplate background check permission form in the resource section at the end of this chapter. It includes basic elements culled from many different examples. Type up the form on your library's letterhead and make sure the governing body of your library approves it before use. You can find many more examples on the Web or in books of legal forms, or you can get them from town or city counsel. Check to see if a parent organization (school, municipality, college) has its own form or even its own policy regarding background checks.

Beyond the background check, it's wise to engage in a little planning and prevention. Sadly, we must make sure that no adult, especially not a man, is in the company of a child in a nonpublic area for any length of time. It hurts to even think in these terms, but it is best for the child as well as the adult. Abuse of a child may be tragic, but false suspicion of someone who works with kids is serious enough to warrant precautions. Parents may become uncomfortable if their child is put in this situation, and there is always the possibility of a false accusation, which, even if it is proved false and loudly proclaimed to be so, can mark a library and ruin a career. In such a charged case, facts are less important than fear to many people.

Men Who Are Not Dads

This rather extreme point aside, we are not talking about regular part-time volunteers doing story hours so much as invited guests coming into the library to share their expertise or to join in a program. The more casual their presence, the more a few men will impact the scene. Fathers may be the most logical source of men for programs, but grandfathers, too, have a natural interest and often more time on their hands. There are men without children of their own in most communities as well who enjoy working with kids— they just never get asked.

It has always been a frustration of mine that, even with my obvious background in children's work, I am seldom invited to help with children outside of the library. I have had to seek out places where I can be a coach or umpire for youth sports, and astoundingly, no one has ever asked me to participate in Boy Scouts, Camp Fire, or any of the other organizations that always seem to need help. When I offer to help, these people usually react with a pleased kind of shock. If you do not know of men other than dads who are working with kids, it probably means there are some likely candidates out there whom you never asked.

How do you approach someone to join a program for kids when he doesn't have children of his own? You could start with the truth. This idea that men are not present enough in the lives of children is not a secret, nor, I believe, is it a minority view. The Million Man March on Washington, national public service spots about mentoring, and Colin Powell's call to volunteerism— all of these carry the message that men need to become involved in the lives of children. Men, like boys, often feel unsure that they have a place in society, in this case a place in the lives of children. Encourage us to cooperate and you may see men jump at the chance.

Remember the literary basis for the term "mentoring." It comes from Homer's *Odyssey*, and it refers to a man who helps to raise Odysseus's son into manhood. Mentor is not the boy's father; in fact, it is the absence of Odysseus in the life of his son, Telemachus, that highlights the need for a guide and advisor. Father may know best, but other men must also be part of your strategy.

Now then, what are some ways to draw men into the library?

BEING WELCOMING TO MEN

We know that youth crime, sexual experimentation, and drug use go up dramatically in the hours between the end of school and the end of the standard workday. The reason is tied to the fact that those parents who work outside the home, especially fathers, are at work during those times. If we want men to become part of the solution, we need to offer some programs outside the standard workday, and they need to be suited to boys and dads. Early evenings and midday Saturdays are the times when many modern dads look forward to being with their kids. They may be pleasantly surprised to find that they can spend that time in a library, a place they do not remember feeling very welcome in when they were kids.

Advertise programs as Dad and Me. I see it so seldom. Is Mom and Me more common because of its alliterative value? If we feel comfortable with one, we should be comfortable with both. Granted, there is the fear of exclusion because more single-parent households have only a female parent, but families these days come in a dizzying array of configurations, so really no direct appeal is safe. And dads are happy to be specifically remembered every now and then.

Invite men in as speakers or presenters, both to get the speakers into the library and to make men feel more comfortable in coming. It is not just boys who see the library as a female-only institution; men feel the same way, and men are not likely to relish the thought of being the only guy in a room full of women.

Highlight cooperative ventures that will interest men. The picture of the modern parent is the "soccer mom" who drives kids around, hands them off to a teacher, coach, or instructor and watches passively as the child goes through the activity. I do not believe anyone is truly satisfied with this arrangement, and men are less willing to spend their often-limited time with the kids this way. Witness the incidents of frustrated and inappropriate involvement among fathers at youth sporting events, the stereotypical "Little League dad" syndrome I've witnessed so often in my years as a youth sports coach and umpire. I am convinced that the very existence of a line separating players from spectators is enough to make a grown man insane. Even when I teach chess, as I will discus later on, I encourage parents (usually dads) to learn along with junior or to take their own lessons. Give them a hope of engagement and they are more likely to respond in a productive manner.

Overcoming Negative Memories, Creating Positive Ones

It seems clear that a better mix of men and women doing children's work in libraries would give a more natural appearance to the library and dispel the myth that reading for pleasure is something only girls do. Barring that major demographic shift, the presence of men from the community in the library will be a substantial help. Whether it is fathers, other male relatives, men from the community, or the occasional celebrity, boys need to see that the library holds a place for them, now and in the future.

We need to make libraries overtly welcoming to males, understanding always that many of them do not have the fond childhood memories of libraries that many women do. Consider a man stepping tentatively into a library, only to find that all the programs are at times he cannot make, or that someone expects him to drop off his kids and sit in a corner until a program is done. Worse still, he feels like he is the only man there. You have just confirmed the early impressions of that man's youth, and you may never see him again. Avoid these pitfalls and you just might get men into the library. Of course, once you get them in the door you must have something for them and their sons to do.

RESOURCES

Applicant Consent Form for Preemployment Investigation and Specific Release

I certify and declare under penalty of perjury under relevant state and federal law that the information contained in my employment application is complete, true, and accurate. I acknowledge that falsification or omission of information may result in immediate dismissal or retraction of any offer of employment.

In consideration of (Library name)'s review of my application for employment, either paid or unpaid, (herein referred to as EMPLOYER) I hereby voluntarily consent to and authorize EMPLOYER, or its authorized agents bearing this release or copy thereof, to obtain a consumer report for employment purposes. I agree that this consumer report may include any of the following:

____Verification of employment, education, credentials, military service

___ Personal identity verification, past employment verification, reference checks

___ Criminal records, civil cases, motor vehicle records

I authorize all persons and organizations that may have information relevant to this research to disclose such information to EMPLOYER or its authorized agents. I hereby release EMPLOYER, its authorized agents, and all persons and organizations providing information from all claims and liabilities of any nature in connection with this research. I hereby further authorize that a photocopy of this authorization may be considered as valid as the original.

Signature of applicant: _____ Date: _____

Printed name: _____

Date of birth: _____ Social Security number: _____

Driver's license number and state of issue: _____

NOTES

1. *Reader's Quotation Book* (Wainscott, N.Y.: Pushcart, 1990), 142.
2. Paul S. Piper and Barbara E. Collamer, "Male Librarians: Men in a Feminized Profession," *Journal of Academic Librarianship* 27 (September 2001): 406.
3. *Oxford Dictionary of Quotations* (London: Oxford Univ. Pr., 1955), 249.
4. Angela Phillips, *The Trouble with Boys* (New York: Basic Books, 1994), 41.
5. Ibid., 221–23.
6. Debbie Abilock, "Sex in the Library: How Gender Differences Should Affect Practices and Programs," *Emergency Librarian* (May/June 1997): 17–18.

Chapter 3

It's Still about Books

When I was a beggarly boy,
And lived in a cellar damp,
I had not a friend nor a toy,
But I had Aladdin's lamp.

—J. R. Lowell, *Aladdin*[1]

As we look at library programs for boys, we have to remember the goal of programming, what we chess players call the endgame. We need to focus on the one thing that really matters when the day is done. We want boys reading. We want boys and books together. Some library programs appear to bear no relation to reading at all, but there has to be some connection. At the very least, library programs gather people in an area where they might pick up a book. This leaves us with two goals for this chapter: to discuss what books boys are likely to choose so that we may build collections that will appeal to them, and to look at the programs that are most directly tied to the types of reading boys do.

WHAT BOYS READ

There has been much study and discussion about book choices for boys, and the discussion has matured over the years. There is general consensus about what boys are most likely to choose, so little of what follows will come as a surprise. Boys choose nonfiction more often than girls do, especially books that focus on the natural world, science, and animals. When they read fiction, boys are likely to gravitate toward books about sports or action situations, and they are much more likely than girls to go for the edgy kinds of comedy. For genre reading, boys will opt more often for fantasy and science fiction. In all cases, they prefer books written by male authors.

Boys also read more material outside the traditional book format—what we would call nonlinear reading—than girls do. This means text that does not flow continuously, such as magazines, newspapers, Web pages, comic books, and comic books' more advanced incarnation, the graphic novel.[2] Though we may know these things intuitively, we do not always have these considerations foremost in our minds when we select books, design programs, or recommend books for kids.

Nonfiction

Studies over the past twenty years have documented boys' preference for nonfiction when they choose their own reading. Childress in 1985, Osmont in 1987, and Hartlage-Striby in 2001 all came to the same conclusion: boys are more likely than girls to pick up a nonfiction book. As they age through the elementary years, all children are more likely to read nonfiction, but the trend is enhanced for boys. This discrepancy appears to be a matter of both nature and nurture. From the earliest ages when children can read on their own, even as young as five or six years old, boys gravitate more toward nonfiction. Thus, the preference begins even before teachers and librarians have had a chance to mold their book-choosing habits.[3]

Then, as children become aware of other people's habits, it appears that boys identify with their fathers' reading, which is less likely to include fiction and more likely to be utilitarian and nonlinear, or even nonbook.[4] Boys then gravitate toward reading trading cards, magazines, and newspaper-like works that give brief information on specific topics. When boys do turn to books, then, it seems only natural that they will gravitate toward nonfiction works, especially those that pertain to people's lives, sports, and the natural world. These topics mirror the prototypical father's reading.

On the positive side, studies have shown that nonfiction reading is more likely to prepare the reader for social and financial success, raising concerns about girls who tend to read less nonfiction.[5] The downside is because nonfiction is often nonlinear, or lacking in narrative flow, it is less likely to produce the social benefits, including language and communication skills, that girls glean from their reading.

Male authors have obvious appeal for boys who are looking for role models. Still, I think more central in the minds of young male readers is the hope that a man writing for children is more likely to understand their interests. Notice that I am talking about interests, not issues. While we as adults may have some confidence in the bibliotherapy approach, boys are more likely to seek escape, or separation, from their problems by focusing on something of interest. Girls are more likely to seek out a book to deal with an issue. If we want boys to read books that address their feelings, they will have to want to read the book for its own sake.

Humor

That leads us to the types of fiction boys tend to enjoy. Although each person falls somewhere on a broad spectrum of reading interests, studies show that the majority of boys gravitate toward certain types of fiction. The more edgy type of comedy, with verbal roughhousing, insults, and irreverent speech, is always popular. Jon Scieszka and Dav Pilky have gifts for this sort of thing, but there are others as well. (See the book talks in chapter 7 and the resource section at the end of this chapter and chapter 4 for more authors and titles.) What can I say? Boys like to see the rules broken on occasion.

Bathroom humor is not acceptable, so boys get a kick out of reading it in a book, and anything gross is sure to be something your mother would tell you not to do, so that's a favorite as well. One of the earliest chapter books I can remember reading was *How to Eat Fried Worms* by Thomas Rockwell (Dell, 1973). Yes, there is little redeeming social value in bodily function humor, but there are other, more destructive ways of scratching this particular itch. If boys choose a literary option, then you have the double advantage of boys actually reading and not playing with matches.

Sports and Outdoors

Action books set in the wilderness or in some crisis situation have great appeal. Sports books do as well, and for the same reasons. First, they have plots that sustain the interest of the reader, making them seem less like work than novels about personal relationships. Second, in their limited experience, boys see sports and adventure as things identifiably male. In these stories, boys hope to find clues to their own futures. Put aside the shallowness of the male experience these works portray. Depth will come in time as the breadth of reading increases.

Amber Brown, the star of many Paula Danzinger books, is a great female character, but we do not expect her to inspire girls to be lawyers. We do not expect every book that a girl reads to challenge prevailing stereotypes and expand gender roles. So why do we expect these things from the books that boys read? One explanation is that we know boys read less, so we want every book they do read to have maximum impact. Unfortunately, this is both unrealistic and counterproductive.

Sports biography combines the best of many worlds because they are nonfiction and often action oriented, and they portray men doing things boys recognize as masculine. They should appeal to librarians as well because once the boys are hooked, they often find the athlete discussing personal issues and reflecting on their relationships. Thus, the modeling extends from the stereotypical male realm into the stereotypical female realm and ends up giving a more rounded picture than one might hope to offer someone at such an early stage of development.

I pointed one father and son, desperately looking for anything that would interest the bibliophobic ten-year-old, to an audiotape of Cal Ripkin Jr.'s *The Only Way I Know* (with Mike Bryan, Books on Tape, 1997). The text would have been too much for the boy to read, but father and son listened together to a larger-than-life "iron man" tell stories of hitting home runs, roughhousing on the road with buddies, and experiencing the paralyzing fear of a wife's mysterious illness. After listening to that impacting book, the son was very ready to find a book he could read on his own.

Fantasy

Fantasy as a genre has always appealed more to boys than to girls. It is akin to comic book writing in that it involves the often-disembodied battle of good against evil, a clear delineation between right and wrong. Heroes win their fame and reach their goals through action—specifically, by choosing the correct course of action. Where girls often seem rule bound, as if secure in the knowledge that order will prevail if it is only given the chance, boys often yearn for rules to help them understand a world they see as chaotic and untrustworthy. The closely related genre of medieval fiction has the same appeal. Knights know what to do and why to do it. Boys would love such a luxury. Science fiction tends to offer more action in return for less epic drama, though these lines are often blurred.

BOYS' READING GETS NO RESPECT

What do these genres have in common? Educators consider all of them lesser forms of literature to differing degrees. "Humor," as Robert Fulghum points out, "is a bit suspect—conventional wisdom says it takes away from serious writing."[6] Still, humor has long been a part of the literary and artistic landscape, and it bridges an important gap. Humor draws from logical, progressive thinking. Puns have to be set up with a premise or an assumption. Jokes must follow a logical course or nobody will "get" them. It takes serious thought to put the most unlikely person in the most inappropriate situation. The logical construct appeals to boys' preferred method of thinking. On the other hand, humor does not operate in a vacuum. If a clown falls in the woods, does anyone laugh? Humor has to be shared, and that makes it exactly the type of communicative, interactive reading that boys need.

Nonfiction is often nonlinear, or lacking in narrative flow. It imparts information, not knowledge, and even less wisdom. This is the same argument against what one finds on the Internet or in hypertext in general.[7] Many educators view sports books as merely visual in their construction, lacking any depth. Action books, especially those set in the wilderness, fair better because they often include personal struggles that involve moral decisions.

Exciting action books may include more violence than many librarians would like to see,[8] but we have to have some faith that boys can see the difference between stylized, fictional violence and their own actions. Boys have an interest in things physical; sometimes that means some level of violence, and it is better to have them explore this through narrative fiction than through movies or video games. Fiction provides context, it gives the reader a chance to reflect, and books do not have reset buttons that erase all the consequences of violence. Still, we often accuse action fiction, especially sports fiction, of being stereotypically macho and lacking any depth. Action books that are set in the wilderness fare better because they often include personal struggles that involve moral decisions.

As a genre, fantasy books never get the respect given to more mainstream novels that focus on personal transformation of a protagonist rather than a physical plot motion. A journey of the heart is more likely to get a Newbery Medal than one taken on foot. In eighty years, only three Newbery awards went to books that can properly be called fantasy. Two of them had male protagonists, and only one was written by a man.

This is not meant to imply that women cannot write fantasy or that girls do not make good protagonists in fantasy. Marion Zimmer Bradley's books are evidence to the contrary, but these factors matter when boys are choosing books. It does indicate that there may be an unintentional bias at work when librarians, mostly female, choose the best books for kids and come up with so few books in a genre that appeals so strongly to boys. It has been more than three decades since a male author writing fantasy with a male protagonist won a Newbery Medal, that being Lloyd Alexander's *The High King* (Holt, 1969).

Internal versus Universal in Literature

As a storyteller and folklorist, this absence bothers me. Many modern "girl" novels are akin to fairy tales, where struggles are internal and help comes from the inhabitants of a parallel world, which implies a struggle of conscience from within. The leprechaun, whose offer of gold in exchange for freedom often leads to unseen and disastrous consequences, is a personification of the acquisitive instinct. Modern novels have the same types of inner strife; they just take out the little green middleman.

Fantasy traces its roots back to mythology which explores the personal in relation to the universal. The struggle takes place outside of the person, and the plot is greater than the individual, no matter how much personal growth results. Do we denigrate mythology? Of course not. So why is the same basic structure considered less worthy as reading for older children? The answer is that we educators believe that an internal struggle has more literary value than an external struggle. We believe children should work out issues at the personal level. While this is a valid opinion, it does come from a predominantly female point of view, and it does put boys at a disadvantage. That is just not how they do it.

If we as librarians were better at holding our noses with one hand and ordering books with the other, none of this would matter very much. However, the truth is that our beliefs about what types of books are "better" have a real impact on what ends up on our shelves and in our book talks. That means that those beliefs affect what reading choices boys have and how they feel about reading in general. Maybe it is because so many librarians, especially children's librarians, are female, or maybe we are just snobs, but we just do not respect the types of books boys like to read. But if you want boys to read, you have to set aside your own preferences to some extent and give them the books they like.

Discouraging Boys from Reading

On the other hand, if you want to turn tween-aged boys *off* from reading, from doing anything in fact, treat them like girls. While that is a seemingly cold and disparaging statement, it is true. If you treat everyone as kids, okay, you stand a chance at making boys feel included. However, do not require boys to read books by women simply because they are written by women. Do we require girls to read books specifically because men wrote them? Do you think boys will fail to notice this? No amount of reasoning that girls read about men by default is likely to counter the clear implication to a boy's mind. You are treating him like a girl. Do not make boys read books they feel were written for girls, usually because there is a girl on the cover. They will assume the book is written in a way that they will find boring or mushy. (And they are likely to be right.)

Most of all, avoid making broad judgments about which books are better and which are worse. Librarians, both male and female, are likely to consistently rank books that boys enjoy as lesser works, and hold up as the best books those that any self-respecting ten-year-old boy would avoid like the plague. Go ahead and hold up the great ones, put them on display and book lists, but do not tell a boy that the books he likes are bad and the books girls like are good. He has heard such things before in different circumstances. With boys in their tween years, the best book is not the issue. What is at issue is what books they will actually read.

Angela Phillips wrote in a touching way about the way boys see such attempts at leveling the playing field and sensitizing boys to the needs of girls. Truly, it is a necessary job, but we should consider points of view as we plan and execute such programs. "It is hard to explain to a nine-year-old boy why girls should have special 'girls-only' soccer sessions while he has to get on with his work. For a little boy who sees that his home life is run by a female teacher, and that girls can read and write better than he can and are far less likely to get told off for their behavior, it is difficult to grasp the concept of female inequality."[9]

Starting from this point of view, any attempt to foist reading on a boy is likely to draw suspicion. Remember, boys have few male role models when it comes to reading. A boy will likely see any attempt to make him read anything as treating him like a girl. It also brings up associations with the classroom which, to many boys, seems like a place designed to frustrate every natural inclination in their bodies.

Remember, boys who are turned off from books always have alternatives. An Australian study published in 2001 showed that even among boys who were identified as strong, committed readers, other types of entertainment, such as television, sports, music, and video games, shared time nearly equally with reading. Furthermore, other types of reading—magazines, newspapers, and the Internet—vied with books for these committed male readers' precious reading time.[10] Attempting to control a boy's reading might encourage a boy to turn away from books to his other options.

In his book titled *Exploding the Myths: The Truth about Teenagers and Reading,* Marc Aronson points out the effect of this control on older readers. "Teenagers are both uniquely vulnerable to the assault (or siren call) of every form of media, and yet they have highly restricted access to books. Adults choose their school reading, select the books for their libraries, and stock their bookstores. And yet adults have much less control over every kind of art, information, and culture teenagers experience daily. Under those conditions, why wouldn't books become marginal to teenagers?"[11] The perception that adults have more control over books than other forms of entertainment probably forms well before the teenage years.

USING GENRES TO PROMOTE READING

If you want to encourage boys to read, then you must allow them to choose their own reading. Start exploring the literature of reading preference and you will quickly see the agreement on this issue.[12] Boys are more likely to become pleasure readers if you let them choose their own reading and give them plenty of the types of books they prefer. Get over the idea that what they are reading does not measure up to what they should be reading; the fact that they are reading at all is a plus, and the measuring stick is probably crooked. Once you have aligned yourself with the books boys read, and with all the other kinds of reading they do, then it is time to start programming in ways that will encourage boys to read with you.

Sports Programs

A 1984 study by Mary Alice Wheeler points out two changes in the reading habits of boys that point to using sports as a vehicle to bring them into the library. First, around the time boys reach fourth grade they become so busy with activities, primarily sports, that they run out of time for fiction reading. Indeed, parents told Wheeler that at bedtime, the traditional time for fiction reading, their boys were more likely to collapse into bed exhausted. At the same time, boys are interested in nonbook types of reading, such as baseball cards and collectors manuals or newspapers and magazines, all of which provide sports news.[13] If libraries lose boys to sports at this point, then sports are a likely way to bring boys back into the library.

In the fall 1989 issue of *Illinois Librarians,* Paul Kaplan of the Lake Villa Public Library District in Illinois recounted his experiences with a baseball-themed program that highlighted the fiftieth anniversary of Jackie Robinson breaking the major league color barrier.[14] He brought former Negro League players into the library to speak about their experiences, and the firsthand knowledge many of them had of Jackie Robinson.[15] This program is a great example of why it is so important to have boys in the library. The past came alive in ways that boys would be unlikely to experience anywhere else. The players the children met and the stories they heard are rapidly disappearing from our world. Childhood is too short to miss things like this.

Kaplan suggested having a collector come in to talk about baseball cards or holding a baseball-themed book discussion.[16] Baseball offers a number of opportunities to bring in speakers because it involves and employs more people than any other sport in the country. Only the biggest cities have major league baseball teams, but each team has a number of teams in its farm system, which contains three levels that reach into some very small cities. On top of that, teams have scouts and other personnel out in communities finding and developing talent. Many of these people are former professional players, even if they are not Hall of Fame caliber. You may not be able to bring in the cleanup hitter from the nearest big league team, but how many boys who dream of playing professional baseball would be happy enough to talk to the scout who makes those dreams come true? Indeed, how many adult men would be excited to hear about the inner workings of a sport that interests them? Let the boys see grown men get excited about a library program.

THE CULTURE AND GEOGRAPHY OF SPORTS

Cindy Dobrez and Lynn Rutan built a geography and research program out of the NCAA men's basketball tournament, and later the women's tournament as well, at a middle school in Holland, Michigan. They laminated a large map of the United States, marked where all the teams came from, tracked the teams through the tournament, and researched the schools that the teams represented.[17] In some cases, you can transfer the basic structure of this program to other events. Soccer's World Cup has many similarities to March Madness, with a large number of teams spread out geographically and competing over a long enough period of time to allow for extended reading.

The Olympic Games fit the pattern as well, but beware; many school social studies classes assign projects on the Olympics. You do not want to bore kids with a sports program that repeats what they have already done, and the last thing you want to do is to associate the program with work. Besides, much of the treatment of the Olympics in the press deals more with social and cultural issues than the sports themselves. If you want to do a program on cultural issues, fine, but do not try to disguise it as a sports program.

If boys are interested in reading about sports and are drawn to nonbook types of reading, then their reading preferences are affirmed when they are encouraged to track down stories in newspapers, in magazines, and on the Internet in order to fill in the map and post articles that relate to the tournament. One advantage to sports-based programs is that they can say to boys that the reading they want to do does not have to be separate from the reading they should do. If we can reassure them of this, then we are in better position to suggest reading in the future.

THE LANGUAGE OF SPORTS

Each sport has a language all its own, but probably none so much as football. There is the official language of the rules of the game, the unofficial jargon of commentators and fans, the proprietary language of players and coaches who call plays in a dizzying string of verbiage that is part code and part cipher, and even a nonverbal language used by officials that seems part sign language and part mime. This is language at a basic level, with word origins and vocabulary and proper usage. It is also language that boys can get excited about.

Bring in the high school coach and some of his players for a "talking football" program so they can show off their own language and explain how it works. This is one more opportunity to bring in males as role models, and if some of the males are high school football stars, the effect will be even greater. Have one of the players wave the team playbook in front of the crowd, then explain that they cannot pass it around because team rules forbid anyone not on the team from reading what is inside. (This is usually a literal truth.) The anticipation will drive kids crazy. This will do more to teach kids about the cost of restricting reading than any Banned Book Week display. Have books on codes and code breaking at hand, too. With any luck, the coach might have an assistant or a player who specializes in decoding the other teams' signals.

Build a huge display, starting with a graphic of a football field, and have the kids find examples of the different language elements used in football and place them on the display. Add a few every day, starting at the beginning of the National Football League preseason training camps, and by the time you add "Super Bowl" to the display in January you should have a jumble of words and images that will be both impacting and humorous.

The still relatively new college football Bowl Championship Series is so confusing to fans, and even sports journalists, that many adults in the community, primarily men, would appreciate a large visual mapping of the process and the teams involved. One added bonus of using college sports is that a natural audience exists among the alumni. College development officers have long realized that sports is one aspect of college life that alumni can relate to long after they graduate. Even if you never participated in college sports, it is easier to get caught up in a homecoming game than it is to get excited about anything going on in your old academic department. If a parent's college does contend for a BCS bowl bid, you can be sure he or she will bring the kids to participate in your program.

Fantasy and Medieval Programs

We know that fantasy as a genre, and the medieval literature from which fantasy draws so heavily, appeals to boys, but how do we exploit that appeal for use in library programming? The reading of fantasy literature can actually be an isolating activity. Fantasy books are traditionally written in epic series. A person can read one after another and never have to ask anyone what he should read next. Formulaic in plot and episodic in structure, individual fantasy books can be difficult to discuss in reading groups. Many fantasy readers sink into their reading to the exclusion of other activities, and, while they are reading in great volume, may have only the narrowest reading experience.

Still, the popularity of the genre among boys means that boys are reading. It is up to librarians to make fantasy a springboard to fuller, broader reading and to bring fantasy readers together in the positive library setting. The recent popularity of books and movies such as Tolkien's Lord of the Rings and J. K. Rowling's Harry Potter series, and the resurgence of Dungeons and Dragons and other entries in the role-playing field, have given us great opportunities to explore the melding of fantasy into library programs.

A librarian named Donna Beales put together a program for junior high students in Dracut, Massachusetts, in the summer of 1983 that was a response to the role-playing game craze. She already had a group of adolescents playing the fantasy role-playing game Dungeons and Dragons in the library. She picked up on that interest and created a summer program called Knights of the Ring that was based on the training and advancement of medieval knights. For six weeks during the summer, participants would become pages and squires, then face a test to become a knight. Knighted participants would return the next summer to help train the next group. The group would meet once a week during the summer and learn what it meant to be a knight through research and guest speakers. The program required each participant to learn a medieval skill such as bookbinding, calligraphy, armoring, music, dance, or leatherwork. Some aspiring knights actually made armor from sheet metal. The participant then had to teach the skill to the entire group, which added elements of active learning and presentation to the program.

The previous year's knights participated in planning the final test, called The Ordeal, which included both mental and physical challenges. In the early years of the program, before liability issues made it impractical, squires literally scaled the walls of the library to gain their knighthood. Races, teamwork challenges, and even a fanciful assault on a giant in his cave at the top of a hill formed other physical tests. The culmination of the program was a ceremonial knighting of the participants, complete with sword on the shoulder and the bestowing of rings. The rings set the knights apart and marked a success born of sustained effort and commitment.[18] Details of the program can be found at www.knightsofthering.org.

As you might expect, the Knights of the Ring drew more boys than girls. The genre from which it sprang made it a natural for boys who have consistently turned to literary heroes, quests, and battles, from King Arthur to Dungeons and Dragons. The program offered the chance to test oneself against an ideal and to gain the respect of those who struggle alongside. Groups have long used this approach to recruit boys for anything from the marines to the Boy Scouts to high school football teams. The program included the important physical aspect to the challenge. It highlighted a utilitarian type of reading for completion of tasks, and it did so within a topic that many boys would find interesting, bridging the gap with reading for pleasure.

VARIATIONS ON THE THEME

As wonderfully designed as the Knights of the Ring program itself was, it is most important to see how the aspects of programming meshed so well with the learning style and interests of boys. The program can then be replicated, the setting changed, the length altered, the challenge reinvented to fit any number of situations. Using the action-adventure genre, a library army of readers could go through boot camp, or the library could hold its own police cadet academy. Tweens could become trail guides based on outdoor adventure books. Using sports books as a springboard, a library could go through a football-style training camp.

The Knights of the Ring points out the power of working as a team through some ordeal to emerge at the other end a better individual and a member of something bigger. The format is appealing to boys, who want to fit in but also want to stand above the crowd. Add a setting that parallels boys' reading interests and the library has accomplished what programming is designed to do—that is, to put people, in this case boys, together with books.

Now turn these aspects of the Knights of the Ring to the classic Lord of the Rings fantasy or the modern Harry Potter series. Each includes a journey or quest, skills to be mastered, opportunities for teamwork, evil adversaries, and points of character to be explored. A Harry Potter program can include advancement by grade; programs on horticulture, chemistry, or cooking (herbology and potions); mock Quidditch games; House Cup points; and mystery contests to find and defeat an evil Lord Voldemort. Encourage the kids to read other publications that explain the folklore and science behind the Harry Potter books.

Using Tolkien's Middle Earth, set up a map as a large game board. Each time the group meets, have a challenge based on the book that participants must pass to advance. Use arts and crafts methods to create the various creatures of Middle Earth or to turn the library into Middle Earth itself. Encourage participants to read beyond the Lord of the Rings series and *The Hobbit* to *The Silmarillion, The Book of Lost Tales,* and all the other works that J. R. R. Tolkien and his son Christopher published.

Both series lend themselves to trivia contests, with bonus points for questions from the supporting materials. (See the resource section at the end of this chapter for a list of these titles.) Each series has also had profound social impact, offering excellent opportunities to use nonlinear reading. Have participants track down references in the news, in other books, and in popular music. ("Ramble On" and "The Battle of Evermore" are two Led Zeppelin songs that contain references to Tolkien.)

Checklist for Genre-Based Programming

Challenge participants both mentally and physically.

Honor nonlinear and nonbook reading.

Emphasize group activity and accomplishment.

Use experts to highlight artistic, practical, and linguistic elements.

Bring in associated reading, including biography, history, and folklore, to broaden the reading experience.

Use competition to make reading a social activity.

BOOK DISCUSSION GROUPS

Perhaps the purest approach to connecting boys to books is the basic book group, which you can begin as soon as children can read and understand

chapter books. While we would generally be looking for ways to encourage boys to join programs open to all, this may be an instance where it is worth carving out a special place for boys. Consider offering a separate book group for them. The different ways that boys express themselves, which will be discussed in more detail later, will make it difficult for elementary-aged boys and girls to mix well in this format. The more openly expressive nature of girls will likely move the discussion, while the boys hang back, unable to connect to the proceedings. As the children move into early adolescence, social factors are likely to be a distraction in most co-ed book groups. If you do mix genders, consider staggering formats that are more likely to appeal to each.

Then, of course, there is the preconception of book groups as being feminine in their very nature. Book groups began as gatherings of women, and book groups today still draw many more women than men. This is due partly to the structure of many groups: they tend to be informal; they encourage personal reflection over logical inquiry; and, among adults, they tend to read books written by women.[19] Hence, men do not join reading groups in any great numbers, and boys see few male role models for joining themselves. It may be best to avoid calling your program a "book group" or a "book discussion," especially if it differs significantly from the traditional format. Book Quest and Fellowship of the Book draw on the fantasy theme, while Team Read evokes the camaraderie of sports.

Including Fathers

This brings up another consideration for the early stages of planning: the inclusion of fathers and other adolescent or adult men. It makes great sense to have a parent, friend of the family, or older sibling involved when trying to promote reading. Remember, our time as librarians with children will always pale in comparison to the time they spend with parents, teachers, and others in their lives. Use the involvement of others to leverage your impact. Mom and Me book groups have enjoyed widespread success, but the "me" is usually a daughter, and often that is by design. If we make the book group friendly to fathers, with them will come the sons.

When Jendy Murphy did her book group for boys in Albany, New York, she held the program on Saturday afternoons rather than after school to separate it from school and make it seem less like work. The choice makes sense for a different reason as well because fathers are less likely to be around after school. Through thoughtful scheduling Murphy was able to get a few fathers to be regular members of her Saturday book group.[20]

Saturday afternoons for younger children and early evenings for older ones can be a special time for fathers and sons to do something together. Children spend an average of ten minutes a day in meaningful conversation with their fathers.[21] Here is your chance to vastly increase that time, and get dads to model positive reading habits as well. If the books you read in your group turn out to be the only books the fathers read all year, then getting them involved is even more important. Remember, dads are customers too.

Active Engagement

You will find that running a book group for boys is different from running one for girls or women. Boys will be much less able to disassociate feelings from action, as William Pollack points out in *Real Boys' Voices*. Boys prefer engagement, active and physical involvement in the process. They will feel more comfortable exploring and expressing feelings in connection with some activity related to the topic. Absent that, they are likely to engage in activities that are unrelated to the topic.[22] Get boys involved in the book or don't be surprised if they act out in distracting ways.

A standard method for encouraging younger children to react to a book or a story is to ask them to draw a scene. This is a sound method, but skewed towards a generally female approach of quiet reflection alone or in small groups. With boys, who process information more actively and congregate in larger groups, you might want to adjust your approach. It is better for boys to paint the walls than to bounce off of them. A large sheet of butcher paper taped to a wall works better than 8½-by-11-inch pieces of paper. Let the whole group draw out a scene or a general impression of the book. Put a paintbrush in a boy's hand and he is much more likely to talk. If you put a paintbrush in his father's hand, too, and get them talking about books, you can take the rest of the day off.

Do a book group on the hoof. No rules exist that make you talk about books in chairs. Take a walk, especially if the book you choose bears some relation to the local area, its plants, or its wildlife. Of course, be very sensitive here to physical limitations such as allergies, especially to bees. Still, these are planning issues. The basic premise holds: boys will be more focused and comfortable if they are expending energy. You can expand the focus of the book by using a changing backdrop to include the physical world in the discussion. If the book involves a journey, as so many books that interest boys do, then a walk is even more fitting. Compare the length of the walk to the length of the journey.

Reenact a scene from the book. Set up a physical problem or challenge ahead of time and test the character's approach to the readers' approach. When I read Rudyard Kipling's *Kim* as a child, I could not wait to find a box and a towel so I could try out Kim's memory training game. The only problem was that I was on my own, so I knew ahead of time what objects I would find under the towel. I ended up writing a computer game that would choose words randomly from a long list, flash them on the screen, then ask me what words I could remember.

On the subject of computers, write a Web page as a group—something that describes the book. Boys tend to be interested in computers, and men outnumber women in computer fields, so you are likely to have some Web talent among the fathers. If you do have a Web writer in the crowd, that gives you one more chance to engage the dads. If you end up exposing the girls in the group to a field they are less likely to consider, that is an added benefit as well. You will need to discuss what aspects of the book to include in the Web page, including author information and graphics, which you will have to find on the Web. Thus, you have both activity and learning.

GETTING BOYS TO READ ON THEIR OWN

Reading is the final end of all we do. We program for boys so they will read, with the secure faith that reading will improve their lives. We see four-year-old boys cry in delight at an oversized picture book of construction machinery, and yet we know that the odds are that child will grow up to be a non-reader. Now that we are focused on bringing boys and books together, we must look at that period of loss when books first exit a little boy's life, perhaps never to return. Bob Lamm, in lamenting the paucity of men in reading groups, wrote that, "In a better, saner world, all those little boys who love having someone read to them would *never* lose their passion for words and ideas and feelings and books. And lots of these boys would become adult men who enjoy sharing that passion with others inside and outside of reading groups."[23] We turn next to that transitional time when we hope to make boys independent readers.

RESOURCES

There are plenty of great book lists out there, but many of them lean toward the serious and literary, many have little to interest boys, and many are becoming outdated. The following list of recent publications, many of high interest and low reading level, are worth having on your shelves to encourage boys to read for pleasure and to read in volume.

Sports and Outdoors

Matt Christopher. Soccer Cats series:

The Captain Contest (Little, Brown, 1999)

Operation Babysitter (Little, Brown, 1999)

Secret Weapon (Little, Brown, 2000)

Hat Trick (Little, Brown, 2000)

Master of Disaster (Little, Brown, 2001)

Heads Up (Little, Brown, 2001)

All Keyed Up (Little, Brown, 2002)

You Lucky Dog (Little, Brown, 2002)

Gordon Korman. *The Chicken Doesn't Skate* (Scholastic, 1996)

Gordon Korman. Everest series:

The Contest (Scholastic, 2002)

The Climb (Scholastic, 2002)

The Summit (Scholastic, 2002)

Chris Lynch. *Gold Dust* (HarperCollins, 2000)

Fantasy

Tony Abbott. The Secrets of Droon series:

The Hidden Stairs and the Magic Carpet (Scholastic, 1999)

Journey to the Volcano Palace (Scholastic, 1999)

The Mysterious Island (Scholastic, 1999)

City in the Clouds (Scholastic, 1999)

The Great Ice Battle (Scholastic, 1999)

The Sleeping Giant of Goll (Scholastic, 2000)

Into the Land of the Lost (Scholastic, 2000)

The Golden Wasp (Scholastic, 2000)

Tower of the Elf King (Scholastic, 2000)

Quest for the Queen (Scholastic, 2000)

The Hawk Bandits of Tarkoom (Scholastic, 2001)

Under the Serpent Sea (Scholastic, 2001)

The Mask of Maliban (Scholastic, 2001)

Voyage of the Jaffa Wind (Scholastic, 2002)

The Moon Scroll (Scholastic, 2002)

The Knights of Silversnow (Scholastic, 2002)

Eoin Colfer. Artemis Fowl series:

Artemis Fowl (Miramax, 2001)

The Arctic Incident (Hyperion, 2002)

Emily Drake. The Magickers series:

The Magickers (Daw, 2001)

The Curse of Arkady (Daw, 2002)

Philip Pullman. His Dark Materials series:

The Golden Compass (Knopf, 1996)

The Subtle Knife (Knopf, 1997)

The Amber Spyglass (Knopf, 2000)

Emily Rodda. Deltora Quest series:

The Forests of Silence (Apple, 2001)

The Lake of Tears (Apple, 2001)

City of the Rats (Apple, 2001)

The Shifting Sands (Apple, 2001)

Dread Mountain (Apple, 2001)

The Maze of the Beast (Apple, 2001)

The Valley of the Lost (Apple, 2001)

Return to Del (Scholastic, 2001)

J. K. Rowling. Harry Potter series:

Harry Potter and the Sorcerer's Stone (Scholastic, 1998)

Harry Potter and the Chamber of Secrets (Scholastic, 1999)

Harry Potter and the Prisoner of Azkaban (Scholastic, 1999)

Harry Potter and the Goblet of Fire (Scholastic, 2000)

Quidditch through the Ages (Scholastic, 2001)

Fantastic Beasts and Where to Find Them (Scholastic, 2001)

Allan Zola Kronzek. *The Sorcerer's Companion: A Guide to the Magical World of Harry Potter* (Broadway, 2001)

David Colbert. *The Magical Worlds of Harry Potter* (Lumina, 2001)

Roger Highfield. *The Science of Harry Potter: How Magic Really Works* (Viking, 2002)

J. R. R. Tolkien. Lord of the Rings series:

The Fellowship of the Ring (Houghton Mifflin, 1988)

The Two Towers (Houghton Mifflin, 1988)

The Return of the King (Houghton Mifflin, 1988)

J. R. R. Tolkien. The History of Middle Earth series:

The Book of Lost Tales (Del Rey, 1992)

The Book of Lost Tales 2 (Houghton Mifflin, 1984)

The Lays of Beleriand (Houghton Mifflin, 1985)

The Shaping of Middle Earth (Houghton Mifflin, 1986)

The Lost Road and Other Writings (Houghton Mifflin, 1987)

The Return of the Shadow (Houghton Mifflin, 1989)

Treason of Isengard (Houghton Mifflin, 1989)

The War of the Ring (Houghton Mifflin, 1990)

Sauron Defeated (Houghton Mifflin, 1992)

Morgoth's Ring (Houghton Mifflin, 1993)

The War of the Jewels (Houghton Mifflin, 1994)

The Peoples of Middle Earth (Houghton Mifflin, 1996)

J. R. R. Tolkien. *The Hobbit* (Ballantine, 1999)

J. R. R. Tolkien. *The Silmarillion* (Mariner, 2001)

Science Fiction

Bruce Coville. Alien Adventures series:

Aliens Ate My Homework (Minstrel, 1993)

I Left My Sneakers in Dimension X (Minstrel, 1994)

The Search for Snout (Minstrel, 1995)

Aliens Stole My Body (Minstrel, 1998)

Lawrence David. Cupcaked Crusader series:

>*Horace Splattly: The Cupcaked Crusader* (Puffin, 2002)
>
>*When Second Graders Attack* (Puffin, 2002).

Jon Scieszka. The Time Warp Trio series:

>*Knights of the Kitchen Table* (Viking, 1991)
>
>*The Not-So-Jolly Roger* (Viking, 1991)
>
>*The Good, the Bad, and the Goofy* (Viking, 1992)
>
>*Your Mother Was a Neanderthal* (Viking, 1993),
>
>*2095* (Viking, 1995)
>
>*Tut Tut* (Viking, 1996)
>
>*Summer Reading Is Killing Me* (Viking, 1998)
>
>*It's All Greek to Me* (Viking, 1999)
>
>*See You Later, Gladiator* (Viking, 2000)
>
>*Sam Samurai* (Viking, 2001)
>
>*Hey Kid, Want to Buy a Bridge?* (Viking, 2002)
>
>*Viking It and Liking It* (Viking, 2002)

Humor

Ken Roberts. *The Thumb in the Box* (Douglas & McIntyre, 2001)

David Elliott. *The Transmogrification of Roscoe Wizzle* (Candlewick, 2001)

Dav Pilky. Captain Underpants series:

>*The Adventures of Captain Underpants: An Epic Novel* (Little Apple, 1997)
>
>*Captain Underpants and the Attack of the Talking Toilets* (Little Apple, 1999)
>
>*Captain Underpants and the Invasion of the Incredibly Naughty Cafeteria Ladies from Outer Space (and the Subsequent Assault of Equally Evil Lunchroom Zombie Nerds)* (Little Apple, 1999)
>
>*Captain Underpants and the Perilous Plot of Professor Poopypants* (Blue Sky, 2000)
>
>*Captain Underpants and the Wrath of the Wicked Wedgie Woman* (Blue Sky, 2001)

Mystery and Suspense

Bruce Hale. Chet Gecko, Private Eye series:

The Chameleon Wore Chartreuse (Harcourt, 2000)

The Mystery of Mr. Nice (Harcourt, 2000)

Farewell, My Lunchbag (Harcourt, 2001)

The Big Nap (Harcourt, 2001)

The Hamster of the Baskervilles (Harcourt, 2002)

This Gum for Hire (Harcourt, 2002)

Lemony Snicket. A Series of Unfortunate Events series:

The Bad Beginning (HarperCollins, 1999)

The Reptile Room (HarperCollins, 1999)

The Wide Window (HarperCollins, 2000)

The Miserable Mill (HarperCollins, 2000)

The Austere Academy (HarperCollins, 2000)

The Ersatz Elevator (HarperCollins, 2001)

The Vile Village (HarperCollins, 2001)

The Hostile Hospital (HarperCollins, 2001)

The Carnivorous Carnival (HarperCollins, 2002)

Peter Lerangis. Abracadabra! series:

Poof! Rabbits Everywhere! (Scholastic, 2002)

Boo! Ghosts in the School! (Scholastic, 2002)

Presto! Magic Treasure! (Scholastic, 2002)

Yeeps: Secret in the Statue! (Scholastic, 2002)

Darren Shan. Cirque Du Freak: The Saga of Darren Shan series:

Cirque Du Freak (Little, Brown, 2001)

The Vampire's Assistant (Little, Brown, 2001)

Tunnels of Blood (Little, Brown, 2002)

Vampire Mountain (Little, Brown, 2002)

NOTES

1. *Pocket Book of Quotations* (New York: Pocket Books, 1952), 21.
2. See Alleen Pace Nielsen, "It's Deja Vu All Over Again!" *School Library Journal* 47 (March 2001): 49–50. Also Susan Ashby, "Reading Doesn't Have to Damage

Your Street Cred," *Youth Studies Australia* 17 (March 1998): 46. Also Deborah Langerman, "Books and Boys: Gender Preferences and Book Selection," *School Library Journal* 36 (March 1990): 132–36.

3. Langerman. "Books and Boys," 134.
4. Karen Hartlage-Striby, "Girls Choose Fiction; Boys Choose Non-Fiction," *Kentucky Libraries* 65 (fall 2001): 36–38.
5. Debbie Abilock, "Sex in the Library: How Gender Differences Should Affect Practices and Programs," *Emergency Librarian* (May/June 1997): 17.
6. Walt Crawford and Michael Gorman, *Future Libraries: Dreams, Madness, and Reality* (Chicago: American Library Assn., 1995).
7. Robert Fulghum, *It Was on Fire When I Lay Down on It* (New York: Villard, 1989), 217.
8. Ray Nicolle, "Boys and the Five-Year Void," *School Library Journal* 35 (March 1989): 130.
9. Angela Phillips, *The Trouble with Boys* (New York: Basic Books, 1994), 227.
10. Kristina Love and Julie Hamston, "Out of the Mouths of Boys: A Profile of Boys Committed to Reading," *Australian Journal of Language and Literacy* 24 (February 2001): 31.
11. Marc Aronson, *Exploding the Myths: The Truth about Teenagers and Reading* (Lantham, Md.: Scarecrow, 2001), 41.
12. Stephen Krashen, *The Power of Reading: Insights from the Research* (Englewood, Colo.: Libraries Unlimited, 1993): 42–44.
13. Langerman, "Books and Boys," 135.
14. Paul Kaplan, "The Boys and Girls of Summer: Baseball Theme Programming Tips to Catch Young Readers," *Illinois Libraries* 81 (fall 1999): 214–17.
15. Ibid., 215–17.
16. Ibid., 214–15.
17. Cindy Dobrez and Lynn Rutan, "Mapping March Madness: Here's a Sneaky Way to Lure Kids (Especially Boys) into the Library," *School Library Journal* 48 (February 2002): 43.
18. Donna Beales, *Knights of the Ring: How to Build an Enthusiastic Junior Friends of the Library Group in Six Weeks . . . and Make It Last* (Lowell, Mass.: DLB, 1997)
19. Bob Lamm, "Reading Groups: Where Are All the Men?" *Publishers Weekly* 243 (November 18, 1996): 48.
20. Jendy Murphy, "Boys Will Be Boys: A Public Librarian Leads Her First Book Group for the Opposite Sex," *School Library Journal* 47 (January 2001): 31.
21. Stan Steiner, "Where Have All the Men Gone? Male Role Models in the Reading Crisis," *PNLA Quarterly* 64 (summer 2000): 17.
22. William Pollack, *Real Boys' Voices* (New York: Random House, 2000), xxvii–xxix.
23. Lamm, "Reading Groups," 48.

Chapter 4

From Story Hour to Independent Reading

The imagination of a boy is healthy, and the mature imagination of a man is healthy, but there is a space of life between . . .

—John Keats, *Endymion*[1]

No one is surprised to see a preschool story hour that is half boys, but you could not fail to notice a program for ten- or eleven-year-olds that was split evenly between the genders. The boys are gone by then, and we are not likely to get them back anytime soon. In the interim, all the reasons boys have to stop reading and to stop coming to the library—reasons such as peer pressure, the challenge of schoolwork, and activities such as sports—have started to take hold.

Peer pressure is a strong force we must fight, and use, when trying to encourage boys to read. Until they start school, children are likely to be in groups dominated by adults. The other children they are with can be of various ages and can range from siblings to playmates to neighbors. Then they go to school and are placed in a classroom where they outnumber adults by as many as twenty to one and where all the children are the same age. Children do not have peers in any meaningful sense of the word until they start school.

When children separate naturally into gender groups, girls have less of an adjustment because they have been spending time with other females all

44

along. For boys, this is probably the first male-orientated grouping they have ever seen, so it stands to reason that this experience will have a greater effect on them. It also stands to reason that boys will have few skills to deal with this new form of socialization. When would most boys have seen males socializing in a peer group? Many male social activities are not considered appropriate for small children because of their context, safety issues, or the lateness of the hour. The few opportunities boys have to see men interact do not generally involve books, but sports or other types of active competition.

When boys gather in a peer group for the first time, the only models they have to work from are those few occasions they have spent with males in their own lives and the pictures they have absorbed from the media. They are not basing their activities on family reading time or story time at the library; females probably dominated these experiences.

Children engage in a broad spectrum of activities once school starts. Many are school-related, and others take advantage of the fact that school children are already on scheduled days. In many suburban and bedroom communities, activities can become overwhelming as parents try to supplement a child's days with sports, music, karate, art, scouting, cheerleading, dance, and so on. In inner cities there are intervention programs, extended-day programs, sports, ethnic activities such as Hebrew, Arabic, or Chinese school, and more. These are unquestionably worthwhile, especially in the inner city, where positive after-school activities are vital to the health and development of children, and far too many children are not thusly engaged. Still, for the children whose lives have become a day planner's nightmare, it can be difficult to get their attention long enough to put a book in their hands.

We have seen that girls advance faster than boys, on average, through the early years of schooling. One classic chicken-and-egg argument maintains that girls read more so they do better in school, and because they do better in school their schoolwork takes less time and they have more time to read. The more that schoolwork is a struggle, the less likely children are to read for pleasure.

We must recognize the reasons why boys do not read or visit the library if we hope to counter them. Peer pressure is still in a fledgling stage, so this is an opportune time to create a group experience in the library, while the peer experience is still malleable. If boys are struggling with school, bring the library into the school experience as a familiar, fun part of learning. And if boys are being overwhelmed by activities from sports to karate to music lessons, it is vital to give them reading that lightens their days.

THE CAPTIVE AUDIENCE APPROACH

If boys tend to opt away from libraries in the early elementary years, it would seem only natural to bring the library to where we know the boys will be. It is important not to let boys lose the "feel" of the library. So, if they will not choose to be a part of the library, get them when they are in a captive audience, preferably one with other boys.

Boy Scouts

The Boy Scouts have activities at different levels throughout the year that require background study. There is even a reading merit badge for those at the senior level. The badge requires the Scout to obtain a library card, do some reading, and discuss the reading with an adult. Librarians are specifically mentioned in the badge requirements, so get the requirements ahead of time and be ready. The badge also requires candidates to perform reading-related service, such as reading to the elderly and young children or volunteering in a school or public library.[2] If an entire troop is working on the same merit badge, the troop can execute a fairly major service project. In any case, getting Boy Scouts working with younger children is one more way to emphasize a male presence in the library.

Younger levels in the Boy Scouts also promote reading. Tiger Cubs, the youngest of them, are required to fulfill a number of electives, one of which is called Reading Fun. The Tiger Cub must share a story with his adult partner, either reading the story himself or listening to the adult read.[3] The child can earn points toward a "Tiger Track" bead each time he completes the elective, so a den (the smallest unit in scouting) can come to the library on a regular basis to improve their reading and earn their rewards.[4]

Wolf Scouts, one of the three Cub Scout levels for boys aged seven to ten, complete electives in order to earn arrow points. One elective, called Books, Books, Books, requires the Wolf Scout to get a library card, list four kinds of books that interest him, read and discuss a book, and cover a book.[5] This is a perfect formula for boys. Have the members of the den choose a book together and read it; then hold a den meeting in the library so the whole den can discuss the book, preferably with a librarian leading the discussion. Go over how to cover a book as an added activity; it is just the kind of active engagement that involves boys, as was discussed in chapter 3.

Libraries can assist scouts in activities that go beyond reading. One Tiger Cub elective, for example, requires attending a live performance. The manual suggests a small, community-based performance rather than a professional play or concert.[6] If your library is hosting a storyteller, puppeteer, or similar performance, an invitation to the Tiger den may be in order. Tiger Cubs can earn Tiger Track beads by making puppets, learning about animals, or making mobiles. Wolf Scout electives include Native American lore, computers, and foreign languages. There are plenty of reasons for scouting groups to be in the library. Packs and dens form in the fall, and that is the best time to contact the leaders and arrange for regular visits.

Stock copies of the Boy Scout, Webelos, Bear Scout, Wolf Scout, and Tiger Cub handbooks. Families for whom scouting is a financial hardship will appreciate being able to borrow these books rather than buy them. Stock books to support den leaders as well, and try to anticipate their needs. Because Tiger Cubs and Cub Scouts do a number of crafts, their leaders may appreciate both your expertise and a space that you have set aside for that purpose.

School-Library Cooperation

Public libraries feel the lack of exposure to kids more sharply than school libraries. School libraries may suffer from being marginalized in the curriculum, from having their time with kids co-opted for a thousand silly reasons, and from being used as a study hall, but at least they see kids on a regular basis. Students in school are the ultimate captive audience. Public libraries become increasingly isolated from tweenage students as they see them less and less. When they do see these kids, it is often in a strictly utilitarian, I've-got-a-report-due-tomorrow-and-I-haven't-started-it kind of way. A small percentage of these kids come in for pleasure reading, and a small percentage of those are boys.

School libraries, on the other hand, suffer from a constriction of resources. Much depends, of course, on state funding and local support, but in general, public libraries tend to be larger than school libraries and have a broader collection. School librarians tend to be tied up in committee work and curriculum development, stretched thin by instructional duties, and generally slaves to ringing bells and school calendars. Any public librarian who thinks that school librarians do the same job in a different setting should walk through a day with one of their colleagues. The two jobs are very different.

This difference, though, provides a great opportunity for both librarians to work together to keep children, especially boys, reading through the early elementary years. School librarians lack resources, and public librarians lack access, so bring the public library with all its resources into the schools where the kids are. Children attend story hours as preschoolers, but when they enter school they are largely cut off from the program that encouraged them to love books. Even if there are other opportunities to interact with books, valuable momentum is lost.

STORY HOURS

The public library children's specialist carefully prepares preschool story hours week in and week out. Why not take those story hours into the schools and adapt them for children from kindergarten up to the third grade? You need only trade in a book or two for one at a higher level and do a little less preparation on the craft, allowing the students to do some of the cutting or tracing. Most of the work is in developing a program; once it is set it takes relatively little time and effort to repeat it.

School librarians should work to find a place and an audience for these programs, whether that be a scheduled library time or a classroom visit. Keeping that momentum going with a familiar type of program will be very comforting to children and will make the school librarian's job easier. Public librarians can work directly with teachers to set up these programs, but it is better to let the school librarian be the conduit. They understand the school schedule, classes, and teachers, but they also have a focus on reading and a better knowledge of the librarian's role. They can also use these transitional reading programs to offset the growing identification of school librarians as research assistants or technology coordinators. Teachers and students alike often forget that the school librarian is intimately involved in promoting reading. Working with public library children's specialists will reinforce their role as promoters of literacy, so let the school librarian be the booking agent.

And why would a teacher allow classroom time to be given over to a public librarian? Many teachers are just as concerned about reading as librarians are, and most are aware of the danger that boys will fail to develop into readers. While classroom private reading time is vital, it is ineffective if boys do not have an interest in books. Direct encouragement during a special event can promote books to reluctant readers. Also, teachers sometime suffer from overexposure to kids. They get so much direct contact with the same population that it gets hard to make points stand out. Kids sometimes need to hear a different voice in order to emphasize a message. A story hour that brings back fond memories may be just the ticket.

STORYTELLING

Of course, once you admit the principle of school/library cooperation there is no end to the programs you could offer with little extra work. I have always used storytelling as an entry into the classroom, especially the early and middle elementary grades. Many children's specialists are storytellers, or at least took a course in storytelling in library school, and do not get enough opportunity to use this valuable skill. Every school teaches Greek mythology, and every school has geography units on different cultures. These are golden opportunities to remind children that the library is all about a good story.

Boys are more likely to appreciate a story if they connect it to an activity or an event. Many of us have seen boys attracted to storybooks based on movies, cartoons, or video games. We can capitalize on this connection if we can only bring boys into the folklore experience. Teachers benefit from the novelty of a guest speaker, public librarians benefit from gaining exposure to children they might no longer see on a regular basis, and the children who need to start with something more concrete than words on a page get a nudge to begin reading on their own. The boys will appreciate a break in the routine of school, as well. More about storytelling in chapter 6.

CRAFTS

Does the public library offer craft programs, particularly crafts from Native American cultures? Around Thanksgiving, schools everywhere study Native Americans, so bring a public library program to the school. Tell the children ahead of time to bring their library cards with them that day, and bring your Native American folklore books along. You can check them out right in the classroom, even if it means writing down borrowers' names and book titles or barcodes. Public librarians should also use these and other opportunities to cross-promote their programs. It is a good idea to tell kids all about the great things you are doing while you have a captive audience.

Public librarians can tie into school library programs as well. If the school is bringing in an author for a day or an artist-in-residence program, bring the public library's books by that author to the school. Children will be excited to read what the author wrote, and the school library is unlikely to have enough copies to meet demand.

READ ACROSS AMERICA

Of all the opportunities for school libraries and public libraries to cooperate, none can compare to Dr. Seuss's birthday. Celebrated nationally on or around his actual birth date of March 2 as Read Across America,[7] this one day sparks interest among people of all ages in every corner of our society. It is all about reading the books that everybody loves and remembers from childhood. This is the day above all days to work together. As a public librarian, I have run joint Dr. Seuss programs with schools in small towns and inner cities; it doesn't matter. Everybody looks good in a tall striped hat.

School and public librarians each have publicity outlets to raise awareness and create the "buzz" needed to make the day special. Start with a continuous reading in the school library. Rotate classes through so that no class is sitting there long enough to get bored or to hear the same book twice. Have prominent guest readers, such as the principal, the captain of the football team, or the winner of your local or state scholarship pageant. Encourage them to talk briefly about why they chose the book or what they remember about it, and then let them read it to the kids.

Even men who are themselves reluctant readers may be encouraged to read something so familiar if they are part of a much larger production. The more men you have reading, the more you will reinforce good reading habits among boys. You may have to choose a few short titles ahead of time for your guests to read, just in case they do not choose their own or forget how long some of Seuss's books can be. Public librarians can read as well, bringing a level of expertise to their reading that the guest readers may lack. They can also use the opportunity to invite the children to the public library after school.

When the school day is finished, move the party to the public library. There, the whole community can join in. Have more readings, particularly by community leaders such as the mayor, police chief, fire chief, business owners, or media personalities. For once, the fact that fathers of young children are more likely to be at work than mothers are works to your advantage. You can invite some of the dads to come representing their employers. Invite the school librarian to be the "ringer" this time by reading one of the more intricate titles.

Put the library's craft program to work, using ideas and activities from the Read Across America Web site (www.nea.org/readacross). If the public library has public performance rights, show a film or video of a Dr. Seuss book. Public libraries may also have more room and freedom to do big group activities such as a best Cat in the Hat costume contest or a Bartholomew's One Hundred Hats parade. These events are a great chance to teach kids how to make hats out of newspaper and then decorate them in a thousand outrageous ways. I like to end the day with a cake, a fitting finale to a special day that will encourage even the most reluctant reader to open a book.

Events like these help to bridge the gap between the ages when being read to was fun and when reading itself is fun. For boys who are going through a difficult transitional period, inclusion is comforting, and fun is encouraging. Seeing the police chief trip over the rhymes of *There's a Wocket in My Pocket* is both a valuable bit of role modeling and an experience they will remember for a long time. (Yes, the police chief may be a woman, and the children's librarian may be a man, but we are dealing in percentages here.)

Given all the possibilities that school library-public library cooperation offers, why is there so little of it going on? Part of the explanation is bad blood on both sides over differences in salary or perceived differences in workload. Public librarians often believe that supporting classroom work is the school librarian's job, while school librarians believe that library skills are their purview. But restrictions on time and flexibility often make turf issues moot. In too many cases, children's specialists are not given the freedom to spend working hours outside the building.

This is not just short-sighted; it effectively abandons the library's responsibility to boys. If many boys simply stop coming to the public library in the early elementary years, then the library must go to them. What good does it do to put up flyers in your library advertising a great program for boys when they will not be around to see them? Even if programs are advertised around the community, boys will often dismiss them as not for them. The surest way to reach a potential audience is in person, and that is doubly true when there are barriers of perception to overcome. If you want boys in the library, you may have to invite them one at a time, and they are not likely to show up at your desk looking for the invitation.

Fight for the ability to take the library beyond four walls. Look for allies. School librarians may have to address public library directors, and public librarians may have to talk to principals, to help their colleagues gain some mobility. Encourage your director or principal to advocate for you with his or her opposite number. Administrators may have the best of intentions, but their primary job is the assignment of resources, which means they often focus on shortages. They have to run a library or a school with a limited number of staff hours. Make them focus on needs that can be demonstratively met and they are more likely to support you.

Emphasize the impact that cooperative efforts can have. For a public librarian, hang your hat on a guaranteed audience. Even if you spent the same amount of your time programming in your own library, rather than in a school, you would be unlikely to consistently draw an audience the size of a classroom. For a school librarian, focus on the availability of extra talent. Principals are always trying to increase the ratio of adults to children in their schools, and too often they are forced to give up trained educators for aides.

Giving up a little class time or letting the school librarian out of the building on occasion is a small price to pay for having trained public librarians working side by side with school staff.

Make feedback a part of every excursion outside the library. Teachers, parents, other administrators—anyone affected by your efforts—should be encouraged to respond up the ladder of responsibility. If a colleague visits your library, thank not just the colleague, but also his or her boss. If an administrator takes a chance and allows a valuable resource to participate in a cooperative effort, he or she needs to see a return on that investment, not just an empty desk.

Talking Points on School-Library Cooperation

Public librarians have resources.

School librarians have access to kids.

Public libraries need to support recreational reading.

School librarians must use public libraries to encourage recreational reading.

Public librarians can bring their programs into schools with little extra preparation.

Children's specialists need the freedom to be out of their libraries to make the most of cooperative efforts.

Provide feedback on cooperative efforts to public library and school administrators.

JUNK READING

School librarians have ready access to boys, but it is largely in the context of schoolwork. This could be one reason why boys stop reading for pleasure at about this age. Their source for reading has become a place of work. In her book *Reading for the Love of It,* Michelle Landsberg talks about the importance of reading in transitional times, specifically how important it is that kids read anything, even what would be considered well below their reading level, or what would seem to have little social or educational value, at these times. She says that "at crucial moments of change and growth, children often need to fall back temporarily, as though to test the firmness of their former ground before stepping forward into the unknown."[8]

Because boys seem to develop later than girls, they might experience this sort of transition in the early elementary years. Reading used to be fun and easy because someone was usually reading to them in a relaxed atmosphere. Now reading is a discipline, broken down into its components and served up as a test. The fact that this type of discipline will one day increase their ability and enjoyment of reading is a tough sell when they are already unsure of themselves. Few boys will be satisfied with trading in story hour for library skills. To get kids through, Landsberg suggests that children be allowed a wide, nonjudgmental choice of reading materials and be encouraged to read in volume through this transitional period, to lay the foundation for good reading habits and to gain an appreciation for the structure of story.

Light Reading and the Curriculum

This view may challenge the curriculum of many schools. In his passionate work *The Power of Reading* Stephen Krashen argues that free, voluntary reading is the only way to develop vocabulary, grammar, spelling, and writing skills. Those who do not read, and for our purposes that means boys, cannot perform in skills-based language arts programs. They are then consigned to drills and worksheets while more advanced readers are allowed time and freedom to read.[9] Remember that 85 percent of special education students in America in 1994 were male.[10]

This is the age where comic books have traditionally entered boys' reading universe. Light fiction mirrors comic books in many ways, and can fill some of the same purposes. Both offer easily categorized morality, a simple compass for a distracted mind. Light reading also reinforces the structure of story so that there is not a gap between the early years, when being read to was thrilling and the later years, when, hopefully, reading on one's own is a rewarding experience.[11]

When I taught at a boarding school for special needs kids who had been in various kinds of trouble, we took this basic approach not just to reading and curriculum, but to every part of life. Convinced that physical and learning disabilities had mired many of these kids in developmental stages, and that the confusion and frustration of these quagmires were causing many of their behavioral problems, the school worked to keep kids active and involved while they worked their way through things.

That meant playing sports at whatever level they could muster, whether it was softball or leapfrog. It meant every student performed in front of the school every year in some way, even if it was playing an inanimate object in the school play. In reading, it meant that everybody read, no matter what they chose to read. And when I say everybody read, I mean everybody. House parents would gather the dorm together in a common area every night and read; it was bedtime stories for middle school and high school students.

Stocking Light Reading

What does this add up to in practical terms? On the collection side, it means stocking a large supply of enjoyable, escapist books, a kind of comfort food for the mind. This is a special challenge for school librarians, who face space and budget constraints in relation to their specific mission to serve the curriculum. Here, public librarians must step in and help, and school librarians must be willing to ask for help. Public libraries have no restrictions that stop them from buying popular, enjoyable books for kids. Many public libraries create their own rules, shunning series books, comic books, and the types of books that professional review sources generally pan or refuse to review at all. This does a disservice to all youngsters struggling through transitional times in their reading lives, but it appears to punish boys the most.

It was little more than a decade ago when public librarians in the rural section of New Hampshire where I was working were arguing about whether paperbacks were appropriate in the library. That was paperback fiction for adults; paperback fiction for kids was not even up for discussion in many libraries. Just a few years ago, the person in charge of buying children's books for an urban library system refused to order popular series books such as the Time Warp Trio and the Magic Tree House. In each case, the material was thought to be unproductive and even harmful to children. Librarians might wish that every book would change a child's life, but it is not going to happen. Reading will change children's lives, but we have to get them to read, and that sometimes takes baby steps.

Promoting Light Reading

Even when they have "junk" reading on the shelves, librarians need to promote it, to put it forward and place it in the hands of kids who are not interested in more literary works. Where do you shelve your series books—or your paperbacks in general? For many public libraries, valuable display space is filled almost entirely with thick hardcover books with big silver or gold seals on them, signifying some literary award. The avid readers who want this sort of thing will go find it. The reluctant readers—those who are there because they are looking for escape or because some adult told them to go get a book—are not going to choose those books and probably are not going to look around for something they want.

Do you book talk series books? What about books on haunted houses or the Loch Ness monster? When you do a summer reading program, do you limit the acceptable books for certain ages by size or reading level? For school librarians, when you bring classes to the public library to pick out books, do you restrict series books or define a reading level for acceptable books? Children, particularly boys, are likely to be drawn to junk reading because they are having trouble transitioning to a new stage of development. If they are told that the reading they want to do is bad or wrong, they are, in effect, being encouraged to abandon reading in general.

CREATING A COMFORT ZONE

The transition from listener to independent reader is a crucial and difficult time, especially for boys, who transition later than girls and are less sure of their place to begin with. Comfort and familiarity will go a long way toward alleviating the insecurity that comes with being in a new setting and having a new set of expectations. Revive the comforting feeling of a story hour for children who have been thrust into school and have found out that reading is work. Provide books that remind children that reading can be fun. Most of all, be a presence in the child's new world. When they enter school, boys are as comfortable in the library as they ever will be. Keep that connection alive and strong by being a presence in their lives, in their schools, and in the activities that fill their time. In the end, you will have more independently reading boys to work with in later years.

RESOURCES

Boy Scout Books

The major suppliers do not carry Boy Scout manuals, and you cannot order them through the Boy Scouts Web page, but see www.scoutstuff.org for prices and listings of suppliers in your area. There are many merit badge requirement books and pamphlets there as well.

Boy Scout Handbook (Boy Scouts of America, 1998)

Boy Scout Requirements, 2002 (Boy Scouts of America, 2002)

Cub Scout Tiger Cub Handbook (Boy Scouts of America, 2001)

Bear Cub Scout Book (Boy Scouts of America, 2001)

Wolf Cub Scout Book (Boy Scouts of America, 2001)

Webelos Scout Book (Boy Scouts of America, 2001)

NOTES

1. *Oxford Dictionary of Quotations* (London: Oxford Univ. Pr., 1955), 284.
2. *Boy Scout Requirements,* 2002 (Irving, Tex.: Boy Scouts of America, 2002), 152–53.
3. *Cub Scout Tiger Cub Handbook* (Irving, Tex.: Boy Scouts of America, 2001), 91–92.
4. Ibid., 71.
5. *Wolf Cub Scout Book* (Irving, Tex.: Boy Scouts of America, 2001), 136–39.
6. *Cub Scout Tiger Cub Handbook,* 123–24.
7. Read Across America, available at http://www.nea.org/readacross/. Accessed July 30, 2002.
8. Michelle Landsberg, *Reading for the Love of It: Best Books for Young Readers* (New York: Prentice-Hall, 1987), 232.
9. Stephen Krashen, *The Power of Reading: Insights from the Research* (Englewood, Colo.: Libraries Unlimited, 1993), see chap. 1.
10. Angela Phillips, *The Trouble with Boys* (New York: Basic Books, 1994), 19.
11. Landsberg, *Reading for the Love of It,* 233.

Chapter 5

Chess, Games, and Challenges

Chess is a library "natural," especially with the latest research results.
Experimental chess instruction for students in selected New York schools
proved to be a great match for computer age kids, they love it.
One bonus is increased reading skills in those who learn to play chess.

—Peter Jennings, ABC's *World News Tonight*, July 15, 1997[1]

It is so great for my son to see a man who reads. I remember the comment so well. It came just weeks after I joined the Parlin Library in Everett, Massachusetts, as children's library supervisor, and a few minutes after a story hour broke up. Sadly, this woman was not a single mom; the boy's father was around, but just was not reading. One has to wonder if the boy's wife will one day make the same observation about her own son to a children's librarian twenty years down the road.

These situations, where modeling of positive reading habits is so patently necessary, form the greatest motivation to develop library programs with boys specifically in mind. While illiteracy remains a frightening challenge in our television generation, it is nowhere near the threat to our culture that aliteracy is. Aliteracy, declining to read even when the skills are present, has gone beyond an epidemic; it is a plague. It is spread not just through constant contact with nonreaders; it is breathed in the very air. It feeds on the belief that underpins so much of our society that the life of the mind is women's work. It is noncompetitive, passive, and effeminate.

On a side note, I believe that the current state of affairs threatens girls as well. Earlier and earlier in their development, they are being pushed to compete with boys, to assert themselves, and to produce on par with boys in a results-oriented ethos. To the extent that girls adopt this approach, they will reap not only the good, but the bad, including a socially enforced distance from the life of the mind. How do we feed boys' natural tendency to compete and to challenge, allow girls the space to compete with boys, and not breed a generation that despises the intellectual in favor of the physical? The answer lies in breaking the stereotype that reading and other intellectual pursuits are passive and effeminate. Our libraries are a great place to start.

CHESS IN THE LIBRARY

Ironically, it was an effort to help girls compete with boys on an equal footing that launched my most successful programming effort on behalf of boys. I was teaching at a small special needs boarding school when the headmaster saw me playing a game of chess with a student in the school library one day. In his typical fashion, he decided to make a decisive move of his own. He stood up one night in the dining hall and asked who knew how to play chess. All the males, teachers and students alike, raised their hands; none of the females did. He then announced that Mr. Sullivan would teach everyone in the school to play chess, no exceptions, and that he would personally check on everyone's progress. He sat down and I hyperventilated. Of course, he had failed to mention such a scheme to me, and I had never taught anyone to play chess in my life.

I taught a school how to play chess that year, from the basics of the game on up, but where the girls *had* to learn, the boys jumped into lessons with enthusiasm. Winters in New Hampshire are tough on kids anyway, with so many inclement days that keep them stuck indoors, but this was a small boarding school with no gymnasium. The competitive spirit had virtually no outlet for weeks at a time, and the boys always seemed to have the hardest time of it. Chess became an obsession, and, for better or worse, I became a chess teacher.

In my early days as a public librarian in the tiny town of Centre Harbor, New Hampshire, an exasperated dad found his son curled up in a chair at the library once too often, his nose buried in a book. He noticed the chessboard I had put out on a small table by a fireplace and he asked his son to play a game. Dad won, of course, and junior was distraught. It did not help that the father then took the son to task for giving up too easily and not trying his hardest. I stepped in as gently as I could and offered to teach the child a few things about the game, an approach apparently lost on dad. In the end, the boy was more confident, the father was excited that his son was playing something, though I think he would have preferred baseball, and I was hooked on chess in the library.

Now it is not the voracious reader who most needs chess in the library. This boy probably would have been better served if I had brought out my baseball mitt and asked father and son to join in a game of catch. What continually amazes me is the number of boys I see for the first time at library chess programs, and how city boys are drawn to chess far more enthusiastically than the small town boys are. Chess has the greatest presence in immigrant communities and in places where large crowds gather in outdoor public spaces. Country boys probably have not seen speed chess, the rapid, exciting version of chess using a special clock, unless they have seen the movie *Searching for Bobby Fischer.* City boys have probably seen speed chess in the local park. Cities are more likely to have high school teams, so younger children have exposure and even some role models. In addition, it is not just the quiet, studious boys that I see in my chess clubs. Perhaps this is because chess is seen as a boys' game; the tougher, louder, more aggressive boys feel less threatened.

THE PARLIN LIBRARY CHESS PROGRAM

In 2001, the United States Conference of Mayors honored Everett Mayor David Ragucci and the Parlin Library chess program with an outstanding achievement award as part of the conference's City Livability Awards, which recognize programs that raise the quality of life in American cities. Parlin Library's chess program stood out because it incorporates both the problem and the solution. Boys are usually the focus of fears about inner-city youth, whereas the library is seen as a haven for youth and an early rung on the ladder to responsible community membership.

We started a weekly open chess night at the Parlin Library as an opportunity for players of all ages to practice their skills and meet new people who play the game. The response was immediate and so overwhelming that it became a problem. These were almost exclusively inner-city adolescent and preadolescent boys, and when we drew more than thirty of them into one room on the first night, they got so exuberant that the reference staff a floor above could not handle it. To ease the situation, we spun off instruction into its own program and kept chess night as a chance to play that often included an ad hoc tournament. The lessons became so popular that I ended up teaching two of the older boys my teaching methods so we could accommodate all the students who came in each week.

Months of feverish preparation and anticipation culminated in the annual tournament, held for three days in April during school vacation week. In contrast to the sometimes wild and wooly chess nights, tournaments were silent and intense. Family members and other spectators watched for hours, sometimes days. The highlight of the tournament was the awards ceremony, where trophies and certificates were presented, often by the very popular mayor. What a message to young boys, to see the most recognizable man in the city standing in a library, encouraging them to become the best they can be at a purely intellectual pursuit, and doing it in a room full of excited, successful boys like themselves.

Everett is an immigrant community of modest means, an ethnically diverse city in which the public school students speak 31 languages at home. Children are often without supervision after school and during vacation weeks, and they desperately need productive, positive activities during the times when youth are at the greatest risk. From January 2000 through May 2001, the Parlin Library offered more than 140 chess programs, including more than 150 hours of free chess lessons. The programs drew some 1,300 participants overall, almost entirely boys.

Why choose chess as a vehicle? Kids who play chess are more likely to score higher on standardized tests like the SAT.[2] The *Christian Science Monitor* reported on studies showing that "exposure to chess enhances memory, boosts spatial and numerical skills, increases problem-solving capabilities, and strengthens logical thinking."[3] Add to these purely intellectual advantages the great socialization factor, and chess becomes an avenue of outreach that every library should consider. Chess also has a humanizing effect for library staff members. Like police playing midnight basketball with at-risk teens, a library chess program creates an avenue of exposure for the library, welcoming children and families into a fun atmosphere, cementing a relationship before the library's other services are needed.

Finding Chess Teachers

So how do you start a chess program in your own library—especially if you have never taught or even played the game yourself? The most obvious sources of help are your state or regional chess federation and your local scholastic chess team, if one exists. Ideally, you will find someone who will teach a workshop to jump-start your program or who will come weekly to play with the kids and maybe give a few lessons.

If your library can afford to pay someone to come in and teach on a regular basis, fine, but that is not always possible. Chess teachers are rare and generally very expensive. Often they are masters (an official term denoting a certain level of success in official chess tournaments) who make a living playing chess. Most take the game very seriously and are hesitant to work with children, especially in large groups. Those teachers who do work well with children probably have their hands full with other clubs or school chess teams, but are the ones you want. Bribe them with the opportunity to look over and develop new talent. All chess teachers are looking for the next Bobby Fischer.

You can leverage your efforts, or the efforts of your teacher, by inviting a few adult men to participate just as players and role models. Recruit them from among the dads, or mine them from the local adult or high school chess clubs. Even if you do recruit others to play and teach, you may end up running the program yourself, and that is probably best. You can keep it focused on fun, learning, and socialization in a healthy environment.

Starting a Chess Program

So now it's up to you to run a program, possibly without any experience or help from the outside. You can still do it. Start by creating a space for the game, gathering a few boards, and advertising a time for players to come. If you schedule the program after parents get home from work on a weeknight, you stand a good chance of getting fathers to come with their kids. Get your local chess federation to help with publicity; most of them have listings of where and when people can play. When you set up your space, remember that younger players must be able to see and reach the entire board. The smaller and shorter the tables you set up, the better. If you can set up one board per table, that is best.

Leave room for spectators. Chess can be a grueling game, even for those who play it a great deal. Do not expect younger players to sit quietly for two hours playing game after game. They are going to want to watch, and watching a good game of chess is a valuable learning experience. If you are a beginning player, you can learn by watching as well. Still, even beginners can play and compete, and have fun doing it.

Learning the Basics

So you have some players coming to chess night, including some very young ones. What do you do with them, especially if you are a beginning player yourself? There are a number of drills, loosely described as "skills games," that break the game down into components that beginners can handle. The added advantage for you is that you can sharpen your skills while not letting on how much you still need to learn.

Start by learning how pawns work and where on the board they start the game. Any beginning chess book can show you, and I have listed some good ones at the end of this chapter. Set up a board cleared of all the pieces except the pawns, with the pawns in their proper starting positions. White goes first, and the players alternate moves with the simple goal of getting as many pawns across the board as possible, capturing your opponent's pieces along the way. The first player to reach the end of the board with a pawn wins.

This simple game can be learned in minutes and played immediately. It is a valuable learning tool for the beginner and great practice for the experienced player. It teaches some very basic points: that there can be only one piece on any given square, that players alternate turns, and that you can capture your opponent's pieces and take them off the board.

The next week, learn how rooks work. Set up a board with the two white rooks and the eight black pawns, each in the position they will occupy at the start of a real game. The player using his pawns must try to maneuver them to the eighth rank, while the player with the rooks simply tries to capture the pawns without losing his rooks. If a black pawn reaches the eighth rank, black wins. If the white rooks capture all the black pawns first, then white wins. Make sure everyone plays both sides. Next week, come back with the white bishops against the black pawns, with the same objective. Then play the white knights against the black pawns, and finally the white queen against the black pawns.

In a matter of weeks, a player can get a great deal of practice and confidence, while still competing and having fun. Then, you only need to teach them how the king moves, what check is, and what checkmate is, and you are ready to play the game. There are a few other rules, such as castling, promotion, and the dreaded en passant, but these are not necessary to play a game. The important goal is to get the players playing full games of chess as quickly as they can. Take your time, especially if you are learning yourself, and do not stress out the children. If it is not fun anymore, you have done all you can for that session. It is more important that the students come back the next week.

Tournaments

Getting beginners playing is only half the battle. You also must keep those who are already playing interested enough to keep coming back. An occasional tournament is a great way of building energy in your group. I run a chess club that has some kind of tournament just about every week. It does not have to be formal, just a chance for your players to test their skill. You can choose different tournament formats so that even if the goal is always the same, to win as many games as possible, the varied formats will keep the players interested.

The most basic format is the simple bracket tournament, where you pair up players. The winners move on to play the winners of other games, and the losers are out. This has the advantage of being very simple for you to run and for the players to follow. It has the disadvantage of leaving players sitting out as early as the second round, and those players are generally the beginners, who really need the practice and encouragement. A double elimination tournament has a winners' bracket and a losers' bracket, and everyone plays at least two games. Many team sports use this format, and you should be able to get a primer from the local baseball or softball league on how to implement it.

Most chess tournaments use what is called a Swiss format. To understand it, you really should observe a tournament, which might mean a field trip. There are an amazing number of local tournaments if you can find them. Consult your state's chess federation, or check the listings at the United States Chess Federation (www.uschess.org).

The basic premise of a Swiss tournament is that as the tournament progresses, all the participants end up playing opponents closer and closer to their own level. For the first round, match up players more or less randomly. A win is worth one point, and a draw (a tie) is worth half a point. At the beginning of the next round, and every round thereafter, match up players with the same or similar scores against each other. By the fourth round, the players who have won all their games play each other for the championship. Match up other players according to their scores so that the players who have lost every game can have competitive games against each other.

A player is never out in a Swiss tournament. Everyone plays in every round unless there is an odd number of players, in which case one player who has not yet sat out a round gets a bye (advancement to the next round) and half a point. The player with the lowest score who has yet to get a bye is the one who sits out, which is a good way to assure that nobody ends up with zero points.

Another simple tournament structure is the team tournament. Many high school chess teams use this format, so again a field trip may be in order. The basic idea is that you split the group as evenly as you can into two teams. I like to choose the two weakest players as captains and let them alternate choosing players. Have each team decide on an order from "first board," meaning the top player, down through second, third, and so on. One team's first board player then plays the other team's first board, and the same with the second board and all the others. Award team points based on the level of the board. The lowest board is worth one point; the next lowest board is worth two. If there are five players on each team, then the first board games are worth five points. With any luck, the score will be close enough that the lowest board players will make the difference.

Chess Variations

You can mold the game of chess into different forms to make your program fun and to emphasize different skills. I am always looking for ways to isolate parts of the game to strengthen players, and these variations are a great way to accomplish this. They also tend to be a lot of fun. You cannot expect players to come and do the same thing week after week. When you feel things are getting stale, try these variations.

MUSICAL CHAIRS

Line up as many tables as space allows with the boards side by side. Make sure the white pieces are set up on the same side of each board. Announce that you will be playing Musical Chairs chess. Have everyone take a seat at a board and begin to play. When each player has moved three times (after black has made his third move) have everybody stand up and move one board to his right. Players on the first and last boards will have to spin around and play opposite their former position. Now everybody has a new position to contemplate, and white moves first. After three moves, everybody stands up and moves one seat down again.

If there is a checkmate on any board, the player who checkmated moves on to the next round; the player who suffered the checkmate is out. Everybody else keeps playing, skipping the completed board. If a board ends in a draw, both players are out. When all the games are complete, take away the extra boards and start again with just the winners. Eventually you will have just two players who then will keep making three moves and switching places until someone earns a checkmate and wins.

What does this variation teach? It makes players find quick checkmates. You have to see the moves that add up to a win and get to them without wasting moves. Otherwise, all you are doing is setting up the next player in line. If you do that on the last board in line and then move to the opposite side of the board, you may end up facing the checkmate you yourself concocted. The variation also makes players look at their position more closely because it changes drastically every three moves. Players have to think creatively in this exercise. A player, for example, might sabotage a position on one side of the board in hopes of being on the other side for a checkmate. The upside-down thinking can be both challenging and hilarious.

BUG HOUSE

Another variation, called Bug House, will certainly drive you buggy. Set up two boards side by side on a long table, with one set of white pieces and one set of black pieces on each side of the table. Two-man teams take seats side by side, one teammate playing white on one board, the other playing black on the second board. When one player captures a piece he hands it to his teammate, who places the piece in the first available spot on the board, working left to right, back row forward. The pieces continue to change hands, but no player can place a piece that results in an immediate capture of the opponent's king. When there is a checkmate on one board, the players on the other board finish their game with the pieces they have.

This variation teaches players to analyze an ever-changing board and to keep their pieces mobile. It also creates such absurd situations as a player having four bishops on white squares where there should never be more than one. Best of all, a less-experienced player may find himself staring across the table at the local champ with a two-queen, or even a four-rook, advantage.

BID GAMES

You can also test the mettle, and the bravado, of your best players by making them bid a game. Take your best players and match them up against beginners; the wider the spread in skills, the better. Have the experienced players bid against each other to see who will give up the most, and the most valuable, pieces. Take each player's highest bid and remove those pieces from the game; then begin. The player who bid the highest and still won his game is named the champion. If the challengers all win, then the challenger whose opponent bid the smallest advantage is champion. This teaches newer players to play from ahead, something they will rarely get to do, and it teaches the more advanced players how to scramble and play creatively from behind.

It also lets the five-year-old who has been playing for a month compete against the big guys and not get wiped off the board.

These approaches should help anyone get a chess program started. Once begun, the success of the program can feed more success. Players young and old complain about the same thing: they never have enough chances to play. Give them a room and enough new opponents and the more experienced players will become regulars. If you can get high school boys and adult men to come and spend time with younger boys, doing something productive and intellectual, as well as fun, you have the start of some wonderful mentoring opportunities, and boys will look on your library very differently.

One note: Chess is such a draw for boys that you sometimes have to make an effort to include girls to keep the program as open as possible. Many chess tournaments set aside a special award for the highest-finishing female. I can easily describe what keeps girls away from chess, and it certainly is not any inborn difference in the way boys and girls think. One of my most promising students was a girl who started learning chess at the tender age of two and a half. She was brought along to a library chess club I taught when her older brother started coming for lessons. While her brother learned, she would often sit on her mother's lap, watching intently.

It took only a few weeks before she toddled over to a chessboard and began moving the pieces on her own. She was off and running. Within a year, she was beating most of the players in the club, including some of the teenagers. She was five years old when she beat her older brother, who promptly sneered, "Girls don't play chess." I never saw her play again. While we are being inclusive of boys, we must also ensure that gender discrimination does not drive girls away.

OTHER COMPETITIVE PROGRAMS

Board Games and Role Playing

Chess is an ideal game for library settings, but there is no limit to the ways you can use mental challenges and the love of competition to draw children, especially boys, into the library. Other board games such as Trivial Pursuit, Monopoly, or even checkers for the younger contestants, may be less foreign to some librarians and still serve the purpose. Hangman, charades, puzzle-building contests—all are engaging and competitive in their own way. Start a gaming club and change the game each week. Fantasy role-playing games continue to have a strong undercurrent of players in every type of community, and they draw on the preference many boys have for the fantasy genre.

Battle of the Books

School libraries all over the country have begun book trivia contests, many of them under the title Battle of the Books. California has developed a statewide program called America's Battle of the Books.[4] The basic structure is simple: produce a list of books, have kids sign up as teams to read the books, and gather for a trivia contest based on the books. Give out prizes to the winners. Be careful when choosing the books not to create a list that is skewed towards girls. You can center the contest on one book or a series, such as J. K. Rowling's Harry Potter series. Just make it clear that you will be choosing some questions that are not answered in the movies.

Mystery Programs

Mystery themes have become popular among adults with the advent of Mystery Dinners, where actors play out a scene of intrigue and clues are doled out during the evening, leading to a race to solve the crime. For a library program, clues can be physically hidden in books, or they can be references to books that might lead a young detective to other pieces of the puzzle. Clues can be handed out at programs, adding valuable cross-promotion opportunities. The East Meadow, New York, Public Library put together a detective club and integrated into it movies, a writing contest, one of those mystery dinners, and even a live police detective explaining how crimes are solved. Half of the participants in this yearlong program were boys ten to fifteen years of age.[5]

Many libraries, library associations, and library systems have used similar formulas to create mystery-themed summer programs, so there are existing programs to draw from. Check with the Saskatchewan Library Association for its summer 2002 program, Uncover the Mysteries,[6] or the Oxford County Library System in Ontario for its 2001 Summer Sleuth program.[7] Vermont and New York offered mystery-themed statewide summer programs in 1998.[8] Many state libraries collect summer reading packets, so check with your state library or contact the states directly.

You can add a little extra flavor to any of these competitions by making them girls against boys. The boys may jump into the competitive part of the program with more gusto, but the girls will be more comfortable working together. Each side then can learn something from the other, and you can never overestimate the effect of a little natural rivalry.

Reading Challenges

The library world has gone back and forth on the idea of reading challenges and rewards. Many summer reading programs log the books that children read, but how do you measure that reading and how do you recognize it? On the one hand, reading competition works against boys, who tend to be less proficient readers and are wary of feeling stupid if they do not measure up. On the other hand, mixing reading with competition—something boys are likely to respond to—may encourage boys to read more. It is reasonable to argue that rewards for reading are a temporary fix and that, in the end, boys will see reading as a chore for which rewards are necessary. But I am more inclined to view rewards as trophies of accomplishment, an acknowledgment of success.

Boys shy away from reading largely from insecurity, the feeling that this is not the right thing for them to do. A well-designed reading challenge can counter this insecurity if the goals are kept in mind. We must convince boys that reading is an acceptable activity and that reading in quantity is, in itself, success. The elements of a good program, then, should include group identity, or reading in concert with others and working toward a common goal. This is a traditional aspect of many public library summer reading programs, but it has fallen out of favor recently. Many libraries no longer quantify reading, or if they do, they count hours reading instead of the amount read. The rationale is that libraries want kids to read for the pure joy of reading, and that time spent in quiet, reflective reading is what matters most.

I hope you see my objection coming. This view of reading is much more applicable to girls. Boys tend to read for more utilitarian purposes—to find out about things they want to understand. Reading is also more likely to be a chore for boys, and long, reflective reading is more likely to be work. Another reason for not counting books is that it encourages the reading of small, usually lower reading level, books, as opposed to the more meaty, "better" books. As we have seen, boys are less likely to be drawn to what we see as better books, and reading lower reading level books in great quantities is perhaps the better approach for boys struggling through transitional phases in their reading.

Still, if you are going to have a reading challenge or a rewards program, it may be seen as unfair to credit a forty-page book as much as one with four hundred pages. One approach that is common these days is to count pages, but this seems terribly academic and laborious for a recreational reading program. My favorite approach is to count books by weight. Announce the Read a Ton Challenge. Weigh in the books kids read on a postal scale and mark them on a large painted scale. Better yet, create an oversized version of a doctor's scale with the sliding weights. That four-hundred-page novel will make a serious dent when it is logged, and so will a stack of juvenile series paperbacks, or comic books for that matter. The leveling effect of the measurement will even allow adults into the game.

When it comes to rewards, remember that their worth is not in their monetary value, but in their symbolic value as trophies. They are a way to recognize a job well done. Do not worry that the ending of one book is the beginning of the next; boys do not think that way. They want to know they accomplished something. They want something tangible as a result, and with any luck their friends will envy their success and want to join as well.

HOMESCHOOLED CHILDREN

Most homeschooled children do not get to participate in spelling bees, geography bees, Odyssey of the Mind, or other competitions that those who attend traditional schools take for granted. School districts may allow homeschooled children to participate, but many parents either do not know about this option or choose not to exercise it. The reasons are varied. Some parents do not want their children in the general school population at all, while others maintain that their choice has made them and their children feel unwelcome in the schools.

For whatever reason, children who are homeschooled may appreciate the chance to experience competitions in the library with other homeschooled children. You just have to find them. Homeschoolers tend to be an invisible population. I have been told by coworkers, trustees, and teachers in several communities that there were no homeschool families in town, only to find that there were dozens. I was shocked to learn that a coworker had called the police to report a truant child who was actually a homeschooled child who was in the library using our reference books during school hours.

In many areas, there are loose confederations of homeschool families that you can tap into, but don't expect to find them in the yellow pages. Many homeschoolers prefer to be independent, and even if they do join with other like-minded people, they are not likely to make that federation very visible.

If you are able to contact such a group, you may have a ready-made audience for your homeschool programs. Once you identify a critical mass, advertising may pull in more. While there are plenty of services you can offer home-school families, a competitive program that mirrors the type of events that produce high energy in schools is a great way to get them in the door.

COMPETITION IN THE LIBRARY

In 2001, chess was banned in the Minneapolis Public Library. The games had been going on for months, organized by the players themselves, with boards supplied by employees of a copy center located near the library tables who saw an interest and a need. The daily games and ad hoc tournaments were drawing diverse crowds, and boys were checking out chess books from the library. Then the fans became unruly, and the library shut the games down.[9]

Fans—chess fans—in a library? What an amazing turn of events. Here was the library, alive, exciting, competitive, and fun—a great atmosphere to welcome boys. And then the library shut it down. Chess was noisy, but was it any noisier than a story hour of three-year-olds being let loose all at once? Noisier than a teen craft program, which would be more likely to draw girls? Noisier than a bridge game for seniors, common in many libraries? All of these programs cause some degree of upheaval, so why shut down chess?

If it was because chess was unorganized and not under library control, then the library missed a golden opportunity to start a new program that would appeal to boys. Of course, it is entirely possible that the problem is one of inertia. Libraries serve seniors who want to pass a few hours in friendly companionship; toddlers make noise; and crafts are an acceptable part of the library world. Unfortunately, that inertia leaves boys, never very well served in the past, out in the cold today.

In 1992, in New Rochelle, New York, a man was arrested for playing chess in a public library. He was not being loud; indeed he was not even play-ing against someone else. He was studying an opening with a chess book in front of him and working the moves out on a board. Librarians asked him to stop because the library had a policy against board games. When he objected to what seems like an ill-placed enforcement of a questionable policy, he was taken out of the library in handcuffs.[10]

Consider the impact this incident has on a young boy who enjoys chess. He sees a man studying and practicing the game in a library. At some level, he realizes that a man younger than retirement age is a rarity in a library. He identifies with the man as a fellow chess player. He sees him exercising his mind. Then he sees the man arrested. What is he to think? How will we ever convince him he is welcome here again?

We librarians need to seriously question the attitudes that underlie the policies we make and the impact our policies may have on impressionable young male observers. Why would we have a policy banning board games? Is it because board games are competitive? We can argue the policy is nondiscriminatory, but boys are generally more competitive, so the policy lands more heavily on them. Do we argue that board games are nonproductive, nonintellectual? If so, how could we enforce such a rule against chess, with all its apparent benefits, but not against knitting in the library? We discriminate subtly against boys by designing a world that discourages the kinds of traits they are most likely to exhibit. We have to face the fact that shushing a boy is different from shushing a girl, that playing hard is not the antithesis of playing nice, and that gluing Popsicle sticks together is not a program that appeals to all fourth graders. If we are unable to make this leap, it will be difficult to see how the library is arranged to exclude boys and nearly impossible to change it.

RESOURCES

Chess Books

Harriet Castor. *Usborne Starting Chess, with Internet Links* (Usborne, 2001)

This is your basic beginner's book of chess. Use it yourself if you do not know the game, or follow its structure if you have never taught.

Nick Di Firmian, ed. *Modern Chess Openings,* 14th ed. (Times Books, 1999)

This is the bible of chess. Although it is incomprehensible to the uninitiated, you should have this book for your advanced players and keep it nearby during chess programs. It lists the opening moves for thousands of games using hundreds of tactics. Once you learn to read chess notation, as explained in some of the beginning books, you can start to use this tool. It answers the simple question, What do I do next?

Daniel King. *Chess: From First Moves to Checkmate* (Kingfisher, 2000)

A very modern and visually stunning book that takes you from how the pieces move to some basic strategy. It also includes a little history of the game. This is a great book to hand an ambitious youngster who wants to read for himself.

Bruce Panolfini. *Pandolfini's Chess Complete* (Simon & Schuster, 1992)

This book uses questions and answers organized under general topics to answer specific questions that may arise. It is a fantastic teaching tool, as students often ask the exact questions answered in the book. It is also fun to use as a trivia game, opening to random sections and seeing who can give the best answers. Pandolfini also highlights issues of etiquette and general practice.

Bruce Pandolfini. *Weapons of Chess* (Simon & Schuster, 1989)

This book is your guide to teaching more advanced players. It contains the most important chess strategies, all organized into short, clear chapters of usually three to seven pages, complete with helpful diagrams. Read one chapter each week; then pull together your most advanced players to discuss a specific strategy. Even if you are a beginner yourself, you can set up a board based on the pictures in the book and understand Pandolfini's clear writing.

NOTES

1. "Bits & Pieces," *Library Imagination* Paper 20 (winter 1998): 4.
2. "Chess Kings: Harlem Kids Score in a Classic Game of Strategy," *Time for Kids* 5 (January 28, 2000): 7.
3. "Kingmakers: Young Players Flock to Chess at a Time When Its Academic Benefits Draw Notice," *Christian Science Monitor* 91 (August 10, 1999): 15.
4. Battle of the Books: Voluntary Reading Incentive Program, available at http://www.battleofthebooks.org/. Accessed August 12, 2002.
5. Frances Plesser, "Programs with Boys and Girls Together," *VOYA* 18 (April 1995): 11–12.
6. Saskatchewan Library Association Summer Reading Program, available at http://www.lib.sk.ca/sla/srp.htm/. Accessed August 12, 2002.
7. OCL Summer Reading Program 2001, available at http://www.ocl.net/sleuth/. Accessed August 12, 2002.
8. Summer Reading Program Packets available at Wyoming State Library. Available at http://www-wsl.state.wy.us/slpub/summer_reading.html#S/. Accessed August 12, 2002.
9. David Hawley, "In Minneapolis, Chess Spectators Can't Keep Tempers in Check," *Saint Paul Pioneer Press* (May 18, 2001): 1.
10. Beverly Goldberg. "Chess Player Arrested for Using Game Board in Library," *American Libraries* 24 (January 1993): 10.

Chapter 6

The Power of Stories

Speak roughly to your little boy,
And beat him when he sneezes;
He only does it to annoy,
Because he knows it teases.
—Lewis Carroll, *Alice in Wonderland*[1]

B oys develop physically a little slower, on average, than girls do. Writing, the physical act of scratching words on a piece of paper, is harder for boys.[2] While this does not rise to the level of a physical impairment, a parallel may be drawn. When children have physical limitations, we try to find ways they can participate that bypass the limitation. That being said, it makes all the sense in the world to consider nonwritten forms of communication when we design programs. This is especially true for the programs that we intend to be noncurricular or extracurricular, as is usually the case in libraries.

Libraries often hold story-writing contests, and these are excellent vehicles for self-expression. Unfortunately, they usually appeal more to girls than to boys, and the boys who do participate are often the ones who are already readers and library users. There are some boys for whom the written word, whether they are reading it or writing it, is a mystery, a weariness, or even an enemy. That does not mean these boys do not have something to say or a bright future with language, just that they need to develop their skills a little differently.

VISUAL STORYTELLING

At the very least, we can add illustrating to our story-writing contests. Boys, and some girls who are unsure of their language skills, may feel freer to express themselves if they can do a significant portion of the job through pictures. We can even run a story-illustrating contest that eliminates words from the equation. There are wonderful books, many written by men, which are wordless or nearly so, to use as examples and encouragement. See, for example, *Sector 7* by David Wiesner (Clarion, 1999), *Time Flies* by Eric Rohmann (Scholastic, 1995), and *Dinosaur!* By Peter Sis (Greenwillow, 2000).

With the help of a digital camera, you can go one step farther and illustrate a story with three-dimensional objects, leaving the flat medium of paper altogether. Boys love to tinker and build. Have them set a scene using blocks, toys, puppets, chessmen, clothing, baseball cards, or other objects; then take a picture. Now have them move the scene to reflect the progress of the story and take another picture. Continue until the story is complete. Then take the pictures and make a simple hypertext storyboard. This is also a prime opportunity to help the kids learn about writing hypertext, and computers do tend to draw boys. Take the first picture, or create a title page, and make it one hypertext page. Make the entire page a link to the second page, which of course will be the next picture, and so on. If you wish to make it look more professional, add page numbers and forward and back arrows at the bottom of each page. You can even post the stories on your library Web page.

The process of creating a story by setting up pictures may sound easy, especially to a ten-year-old boy who has never tried it, but just wait until they do! Challenge them to tell a story this way with a set of blocks, or toys, or a box of everyday objects that you supply. Let them explore the structure of story, the movement of plot, the setting, and the rest, without language getting in the way. Then, when they do approach a story that contains language, they will be more confident of themselves and better equipped to handle the words.

ORAL STORYTELLING

Of course, you can still introduce words to a story without those words having to be written. If boys on average have a harder time with the written word than girls do, and boys are more vocal and physical than girls are, then storytelling is a natural avenue to explore with boys. I am not talking about drama, where the words belong to some disembodied author, but traditional storytelling, where one or two people interpret a story for an audience. It is active, engaging, and very vocal, making it a perfect match for tweenage boys. As a traveling storyteller, I have spent hundreds of hours in front of audiences of all ages. I am convinced that many boys who have long ago lost any interest in written stories may still respond to stories in motion. Boys who participate in storytelling as both observers and performers may bridge the gap from being read to as a child to reading independently as an adolescent.

Teaching Boys to Tell Stories

The first step in getting kids to tell stories is getting them to open their mouths, an amazing thought given that many boys seem so loud and boisterous. However, standing up and speaking to a room full of people seems easier to a boy when he knows he is not supposed to be doing it, like when he stands up on a table in a school lunchroom and recites an irreverent version of some popular song. Actually, what that boy is doing is good training for storytelling. All he needs to make his performance productive is a sense of story, and that is what a good library storytelling workshop can give him.

I have taught the following program a number of times now, always in school or summer school settings, where the audience was captive and coeducational. I hold classes once a week over five or six weeks. Both urban and rural kids reacted with some reserve to the idea of a class in storytelling, but the boys quickly warmed to the chance to speak out. Boys recognize, as we all should, that storytelling plays to their strength and gives them a chance to succeed. In the process, they pick up the structure of story and learn to appreciate language as a tool they can wield rather than a puzzle that will frustrate them. Even so, there is no reason to think that teaching storytelling will appeal only to boys or only to kids. Storytelling is a universal art. Everyone can tell a story; you just have to convince a person that he or she has a story to tell.

Sit the participants in a circle and join them yourself, whether you have three students or thirty. Sit them five deep if you have to, as long as they are circled up. Explain to them that storytelling in most of the world was traditionally done in a circle. Far from the performance art we see today, it was often a participatory activity, whether that meant people took turns telling stories or the audience had a part in the telling. This seating arrangement, and the explanation that goes with it, adds an air of ceremony to the proceedings. It is important to make storytelling special.

Let the participants know that they are all going to become storytellers; indeed, they already are. Not only does everybody tell stories, but we all have stories that are uniquely our own. These first few exercises are meant to prove these points and get the group comfortable with speaking in a storytelling setting. If the size of the group permits, every participant should speak in front of the group every time it meets.

SPEAKING EXERCISES

Everybody is born with a story because everybody has a name. Go around the circle asking everybody to say his or her name and tell the story of that name. That story comprises both the family name and the given name or names. Be careful of the terms "first" and "last" name; many Asians traditionally say the family name first. For the family name, what is the nationality? Where do the ancestors of the same name come from? What does the family name mean in the original language? For many English names, this could be easy, but many names in other languages will be more poetic. This is inherently discriminatory, as most cultures give the family name of the father to the children. You can give the option of exploring a mother's maiden name, but the point of the exercise is to see the story that each individual carries in his or her name.

Ask the participants about their given names. What language is the name from? What does it mean? Why did the participant's parents choose the name? Was there a namesake, someone for whom the person was named? What qualities that the namesake possessed led the parents to honor him or her? Are there siblings whose names are related in some way? Was there some circumstance surrounding the birth that suggested the given name?

Let everybody know what you expect of them, and then prompt participants as they work their way through the recital. Two things will be quickly apparent. First, names can be great stories. Second, most people have no idea about the story behind their own names. Do not push things, especially if you use this as an opening exercise. If someone does little more than state his or her name, that is a good beginning. If the group is small enough, go person by person. If the group is very large you can take volunteers. You should be ready to tell your story as well in order to model the possibilities. To that end, I give the story of my name:

My name is Michael Edward Sullivan. Sullivan is Irish, of course, and Edward is my father's name. The name Michael is found in many languages, but in the Gaelic, or Irish, it means "godlike." How would you like to carry around a name like that? Actually, it is traditional for an Irish family to give the first son, like me, or the first daughter, religious names, with the intention that they will take religious vows as either a priest or a nun. My oldest sister is named Virginia, which means pure.

I almost did not get my name, because it was already taken when I was born. That needs some explanation. My father is the youngest of nine siblings. His sister, the oldest in the family, had seven sons. My parents wanted to name their first son Michael, but when they had first one, then two, then three, then four daughters, they gave up and got a dog. They named him Mike. I arrived less than a year later. Thankfully, they kept me and got rid of the other Mike. I am one of the few people who can say I was named after a dog.

Now send the participants to fill in the gaps in the stories of their names. Have baby name books available for finding the meaning of given names and books of heraldry and foreign language dictionaries for finding the meaning of family names. Encourage participants to talk to relatives about their names. When the group gets together again, ask participants to relate any new findings.

Once the group recognizes that they each have a story of their own, help them to see that there are stories all around them. Go ahead and ask who has heard a storyteller. A few may have seen traditional storytellers, but remind them that stories come in many forms. Ask for someone to volunteer to tell a story; then ask them to tell "Mary Had a Little Lamb." When the laughter dies down, have the volunteer say the words to the song. Then ask anyone else if they would like to tell a story based on a song.

Point out they do not have to know all the words, or repeat them exactly. What you want is the story—a beginning, a middle, and an end. Kids especially like to talk about their music, so start with some suggestions for traditional songs that most people will know, but encourage participants to recount their favorite lyrics. Once again, encourage everyone to think about the exercise and come in ready to "tell" a song the next time the group meets.

Circle up again and offer to tell the first story. Then tell the group a joke. Many people do not realize that jokes, as told by stand-up comedians, are the most direct descendants of traditional storytelling we are likely to see these days. Boys especially will be encouraged to hear that passing on their favorite funny story is actually an art form. Make the distinction between a riddle, which is a question-and-answer sequence, and a joke, which is a story with an unexpected or humorous twist. Then let them loose, with a warning to keep it clean.

I generally begin these exercises sitting down, but at some point I start asking people to stand in their places when they speak to the group. I do not want to break the circle and turn a teller into a performer, but I want the participants to claim more attention once they feel comfortable in the group. It is vital to build some level of trust, which is why having everyone participate is so important. It is a shared experience, and if that is not enough to cut down the catcalls, it helps to know you are next in the spotlight.

LISTENING EXERCISES

By now, your participants have spoken a number of times in front of the group. They have become used to speaking, so it is time to emphasize the art of listening. Remind the group that storytelling began in preliterate societies. People told stories because they could not write them down. Storytellers learned their stories by listening to other storytellers. To this day, many stories are handed around orally in story circles, a concept that will be familiar to your group.

If the group is large, choose ten to twelve volunteers to form a small circle within the larger circle. If the group is small, let everyone participate. Now play the famous game of "gossip." Many of your participants will be familiar with this one, and they will be immediately put at ease. Whisper a long sentence into one person's ear, and have that person whisper the same sentence into the next person's ear. Go around the circle until the sentence gets to the last person. No second chances, no repeating. Have the last person say what he or she heard out loud, then repeat the original sentence aloud. The two sentences will probably be very different. Play the game again, or bring in new volunteers. Make it a competition of sorts to see who can pass the message around with the smallest alteration.

Gossip is a familiar activity, and it sets up a more serious exercise, which I call "witness." Send four volunteers out of the room while you set up a fifth volunteer in a chair in the middle of the circle. Stand in front of the "witness" and describe a crime, including a description of the perpetrator. Throw in a good number of details, and make the description last about thirty seconds. Then call in one of the volunteers from outside and put him or her in the witness chair. Have the first witness repeat the description to the second; then call in the third witness to hear the story from the second. Keep going until the last witness hears the tale and repeats it back to the whole group.

The story will certainly get much shorter as the exercise progresses. Many details will get lost in the telling. Ask the group to think about which details made it through. Usually, these will be the action (plot) and one or two distinguishing features of the perpetrator (characterization). Point out that these are at the very core of storytelling, since they are the memorable parts of stories. Feelings and impressions do not carry well. If any details get added or changed, they will probably be of this type. Discuss what this might mean for storytelling.

Some participants might try to memorize words or phrases, but, as in the game of "gossip," the words get garbled and emerge as different words with different meanings. If action and description are the most memorable parts of a story, then the easiest way to remember a story is by visualizing its progress. Tell the participants to play it through their heads like a movie, and simply describe the action as they see it. Now choose five more witnesses and play the game again to see if they relate the story more accurately.

The next exercise ties together listening, visualizing, and speaking, and may be the most fun of all the activities in the program. Call it "pathological liar." Circle up and start by making a slightly unlikely statement, such as, "I ate twenty pancakes for breakfast." The next person must tell a fib just a little more outlandish, and alter it in some way. No fair just adding numbers; players must qualitatively change the statement.

"That's nothing. I ate twenty pancakes covered in honey."

"Well, I ate twenty pancakes covered in honey, with the bees still in the honey."

"I ate twenty pancakes covered in honey with the bees still in it, and I had to fight off the bear while I did it."

Inevitably, someone will make a statement that has nothing to do with the previous statement, and you will have to start again. Point out that each person must listen closely as the story builds and add a detail that was not there before. To do this, they will have to visualize the action or they will lose track of the story in the flood of new details.

Encourage participants to meet in groups between sessions to practice all these exercises. Suggest that they use the library as the place to practice, to find short stories on which to base their witness games, and to look up tall tales to see how outrageous these stories can become. These are not exercises that can be done alone, and the group work is a vital component for reaching boys.

STORYTELLERS AT LAST

Now you are ready to introduce true storytelling. Once again, start in a circle with familiar material to put the group at ease, and make it a participatory activity. Start with a story like "Goldilocks and the Three Bears." Say ten words to begin the story, counting them on your fingers. The next person says ten more words, and so on around the circle. Emphasize that everyone must listen attentively to follow the story. Not everyone will remember the story the same way. Go around the circle until the story is done. For your next story, introduce a twist. Hold up a tennis ball when you start the story; then roll it to someone in the circle. Whoever gets the ball tells the next part and rolls the ball to someone else.

Next, copy off a number of very short stories from story collections, short enough to read in a minute or two. The fables at the end of this chapter are a good place to start as well. Form a few groups of three or four and let each group read through a story a few times together. Do not give them enough time to script a story, just to read it a few times. Then have the group stand together in the circle and play the same game: ten words and hand it over to the next person. Emphasize the need to just get the story across. Keep going until everyone has had a chance to tell.

You are finally ready to hand out one story to each person. Keep them very short, and give everyone a chance to prepare the story between sessions. Circle up and remind everyone again that the point is to recount the story, primarily its characters and its action. When you get around the circle, you can state that everyone in the room is now a storyteller.

Choosing Stories for Boys

When choosing stories to tell that will interest boys, or choosing stories for boys to tell others, it is important to remember the reading habits of boys. Look for humor and action, even if you do not feel these are the most important elements in stories. Try not to shrink from a little gore. Avoid overly contemplative stories, or ones that deal primarily with internal struggle. Choose mythology over fairy tales.

Balance, of course, is the key. Look at the stories you are presenting, or the ones you will offer the children to tell. Notice how many main characters are boys and how many are girls. Most boys will choose male characters and most girls will choose female; it is only natural. If there are very few male characters, the boys will look on storytelling the way they look on so many library juvenile fiction collections: chosen by, written by, and designed for, girls. Be wary of cautionary tales in their traditional form; they portray boys as devious, mean, and stupid just as often as they portray girls as silly and helpless.

Look for true folktales, as distinct from the more formal, and usually more recent and more European, fairy tales. Folktales often portray journeys of discovery and cosmic themes. They deal with the natural world more than the interpersonal world of humans. They invoke humor, rather than fear, to teach lessons. They show a path to right behavior, rather than brandishing a whip for wrong behavior. Anansi the spider, in so many African tales, goes looking for trouble, and gets into it as soon as he finds it. Anansi takes his lumps and learns his lessons, but he is always funny and remains at the center of things, always in place, always looking for the next day's prank.

STORIES FOR TELLING

What follows are stories that I have developed and adapted with special appeal for boys. Tell them yourselves, or let the children become the storytellers.

Cuchulainn and the King of the Fairy Folk

This story from Ireland is representative of a type of story found throughout Europe, the most famous of which is the tale of the Green Knight from the King Arthur legends. It is also one of many tales of the three great heroes of Ulster striving to be acknowledged as the best. The others are strong, but Cuchulainn triumphs by his strength of character. The story is rife with courage and honor, themes that speak to boys at an almost molecular level, and a little gore does not hurt either. Tell this one with big motions, wild fluctuations of tone and volume, and watch the boys follow every swing of the ax.

An age ago, the biggest troublemaker in all of Ireland was a man called Bricriu the Poison Tongue. It was said that a huge wart would grow on his face if ever he had a secret that he hadn't told to someone. He knew everybody's business and had great fun making trouble wherever he could. Once, he decided that Ireland had been quiet for too long, so he came up with an evil plan. He decided to have a party. (Does that sound evil?) More than that, he decided to have a great feast. He invited everyone of any note in the kingdom, including the three great heroes, all Knights of the Red Branch—Leogaire of the iron arms; Conall Cernach, undefeated in battle; and the famous Cuchulainn. He had a special hall built, because there were no halls big enough for the feast. He filled the hall with long tables and loaded those tables with the finest food and wines. And at the head of the center table he set up the seat of honor, a huge chair of carved wood with the hero's portion of the feast in front of it. The hero's portion was the largest and choicest cuts of meat, the most exotic fruits, and the finest wine. The three great heroes entered the hall, and people began to whisper. Who would Bricriu offer the seat of honor? The heroes all stood near the great chair waiting to be asked, but old Poison Tongue for once said nothing. He didn't invite anyone to sit; he just walked away. The three champions immediately began to argue over who should sit in the place of honor.

Meanwhile, old Poison Tongue had whispered to the wives of the three champions that whichever of them entered the hall first would prove her husband was the greatest and earn the first place among all women in Ireland. At first, the three wives walked gracefully toward the hall; then they began to hurry and elbow each other out of the way. Finally they ran for the door and all reached it at once. A huge fight broke out, which their husbands joined with swords drawn, and it looked like there would be war in Ireland over who was the greatest hero.

Just then, a huge and fierce-looking stranger entered the hall and demanded hospitality. He was twelve feet tall with a bushy red beard and blazing eyes. In one arm he carried a chopping block made from the trunk of a great tree, and in the other hand he held an axe eight feet long.

The room went silent and everyone looked at the giant, who said loudly, "I have come in search of fair play. I propose a test. Let the greatest hero among you step forward, and I will cut off his head. Tomorrow I will come back and he can cut off my head."

As you might expect, there were not a lot of takers for his challenge.

The giant laughed and said, "All right, I will make it easier for you. Let the greatest among you come forward and cut off my head, and tomorrow I will come back and cut off his."

That sounded a lot safer, and Leogaire of the iron arms stepped forward to take the challenge. The giant handed him his axe and laid his head on the chopping block. Leogaire took that huge axe in his iron arms and with one mighty stroke cut the giant's head clean off. The crowd cheered, but then everyone went silent as the giant stood up, walked over to his head, picked it up, and put it under one arm.

He picked up the chopping block and the axe and walked out of the hall.

The next night, the giant returned, his head in place once again, carrying the chopping block and the axe. He called out, "Where is this great hero, Leogaire? I have come to collect my half of the bargain." But Leogaire of the iron arms was nowhere to be seen.

The giant laughed out loud. "Some hero, running out on his word. Are there any real heroes among you?" Everyone was silent. The giant swept the room with his axe until he was pointing straight at Conall Cernach. "You, I challenge you to take my test."

Conall Cernach, undefeated in battle, went white, but he couldn't refuse a direct challenge. He got to his feet, took the axe, and in one stroke cut off the giant's head. He trembled as he saw the giant rise, pick up his head, and walk calmly out of the hall.

The next night, the people returned to the great hall, but there was no rejoicing. They waited until darkness fell, and the giant returned. He stalked to the center of the hall, the axe and chopping block under his arms and his head back in place. He called out loudly, "Bring out Conall Cernach; I have unfinished business with him." But Conall Cernach, undefeated in battle, was not there.

"Is this the best that Ireland has?" the giant bellowed. "Are there no heroes in Ireland with a sense of fair play? Ireland is a land of cowards and cheats!"

Cuchulainn was frightened, but he couldn't allow all of Ireland to be defied. He stepped forward and accepted the challenge. The giant handed him the axe and Cuchulainn smote off his head. He looked on grimly as the giant picked up his head and stalked out of the room.

The next night, the giant returned and called, "Where is this great hero of Ireland? Has Cuchulainn run away as well?" And Cuchulainn stood up and stepped forward. Frightened as he was, he had returned to fulfill his half of the bargain. The giant put down the chopping block, and Cuchulainn laid his head on it. The crowd wept to see such a hero go to his doom. The giant gave a grim smile as he tested the edge of his axe. He raised the huge axe in one mighty hand almost to the rafters and brought it down with such force that the wind whistled through the hall. He brought the axe down with a thundering crash, burying it deep into the wood of the chopping block and cutting off the end of one hair on Cuchulainn's head.

Cuchulainn was stunned. He felt his neck to make sure his head was still attached. The giant said, "Stand up, Cuchulainn. There is not a champion in all Ireland who is equal to you in skill, in courage, or in honor. I am of the Tuatha De Danaan, the King of the Fairy Folk of Ireland, and I swear by the magic of my people that if anyone challenges your right to a place of honor, he will die that very night." And with that the giant stalked out of the hall. No one ever saw the King of the Fairy Folk again, and never again did anyone challenge Cuchulainn's right to the seat of honor.

Versions of the Feast of Bricriu can be found in Brid Mahon's *Irish Folklore* (Mercier, 2000) and Liam Mac Uistin's *Celtic Magic Tales* (O'Brien, 1993), among other places.

Stone Soup

"Stone Soup" is to storytelling what "Misty" is to jazz. It is so standard that you should never be surprised to hear it, but because it is such a standard each teller must bring something individual to the performance. You will find versions of this story under such names as "Rock Soup," "Stone Broth," "Soldier's Soup," "The Old Woman and the Tramp," and even an early American version called "The Rabbit and the Rock Soup." This is my take, and it is unlike any other telling I have found, largely because it is told from the point of view of the settled people, not the wanderer. It takes the basic premise of a soup started by someone with nothing but a stone, or in some cases a nail, and it supposes a more serious, distant origin. Assuming ancient beliefs in hospitality, why would anyone refuse to share his or her food with a hungry stranger? If the strangers were rogue soldiers, as in some versions, surely, but take out that element and you have more interesting possibilities. If hunger is tied to fear of the stranger, it is easy to place the story much farther back, in the days of the mysterious plague that ravaged Europe, and suddenly the story is about the courage to reach out to others in the face of nameless fear, great points for boys looking for a place in society. It is here for you to imitate or use as a springboard for your own interpretation. Try to tell this to the most diverse audiences you can find; different ages and even generations have their place, and many immigrant populations will recognize the story as their own. I think of my grandfather, a tough old French Canadian, when I tell this, and the image of handing down the story and the moral will speak to multiple generations.

Long ago, there was a tiny little village tucked away in the mountains of France. It was a happy village. Most people were farmers, and they would talk and laugh with each other on the road as they went off to their fields. The women would gather each day at a market in the center of the village to sell what they had extra, buy what they needed, and share the news and gossip of the day. All the children played together, and the village had a little school where all the children went. Every spring, the whole village would gather for a festival of dancing and singing.

But when our story begins, the village was not such a happy place. Two years earlier, a terrible sickness had come to the town. They say a stranger brought it with him, because he was the first one to get sick, but many, many people got sick after him. The worst part was, once one person got sick, it seemed everybody he knew got sick too. People became afraid; they didn't want to see other people because that was how you got sick. They closed down the little school because parents didn't want their children getting the sickness from other children. Fewer and fewer women came to the market until it was all but deserted. Men started to avoid each other as they went to the fields. Finally, people stopped going out altogether, to their fields, or to the market, or even to get firewood. When winter came, they sat in their homes, cold, hungry, and afraid.

Of course, there are some people who won't sit in a cold dark house all winter. The children of the village would sometimes sneak out of their houses to try to find a little food growing wild, or to get a little firewood, to meet up with their friends, or to just run wild through the woods.

One day, late in the second winter of the disease, all the children of the village were out running through the woods when they saw the most amazing sight. There was a stranger walking down the path that ran near the village. Now strangers were rare enough in this suspicious time, but this one was stranger than most. He was dressed all in rags, and his coat was so covered in patches you couldn't even tell what color it was. He had a ragged shoe on one foot, and the other foot was bare. And on his head he wore a pot for a hat. The children couldn't resist following him. The stranger saw them dodging behind trees, but he pretended not to notice.

The stranger walked until he came to a little stream, and he sat down on a tree stump beside it. He gathered up a few leaves and twigs and started a small fire. Then he took the pot from his head, dipped a half a pot of water from the stream, and set the pot over the fire. Then, reaching deep into a pocket, he pulled out a small stone. He brushed off the stone and carefully dropped it into the pot. Then he took a wooden spoon from another pocket and began to stir.

The children were so curious that they forgot to hide. They started moving up and forming a wide circle around the stranger. One little boy, braver than the rest, walked up to the stranger and asked, "What are you making?"

The stranger looked down at the pot, then up at him, and said, "Stone soup." Then he went back to his stirring.

The boy licked his lips. He didn't know what stone soup was, but he knew he was hungry. "Can I have some stone soup?" he asked. The stranger said, "I brought the stone; what did you bring?"

The boy thought hard and said, "I think I have a potato."

The stranger nodded, and the boy ran off back home. In a few minutes he came running back, holding out a tiny, pale, half-rotten potato. It must have sat unnoticed in the bottom of a bin all winter. The stranger took the potato and pulled a small knife out of his pocket. He carefully carved off the rotten part and dropped the rest in the pot.

"Can I have some stone soup now?" the boy asked.

The stranger looked into the pot and said, "It's not ready yet." So the boy sat down to wait.

A second boy came up and asked, "What are you making?"

The stranger looked up at him and said, "Stone soup." Then went back to his stirring.

"Can I have some stone soup?" the second boy asked.

The stranger said, "I brought the stone, and he brought a potato; what did you bring?"

The boy ran off back home. In a few minutes he came running back, holding out a crooked little carrot. The stranger trimmed off the leaves and dropped the carrot in the pot.

"Can I have some stone soup now?" the second boy asked. The stranger looked into the pot and said, "It's not ready yet." So the second boy sat down to wait.

By now, the rest of the children had figured out the rules to this game, and they all scattered back to their homes. One by one, they came back with a parsnip here, a turnip there, a few cabbage leaves, and a handful of dried peas. One little girl even brought a small piece of beef, more gristle than meat. Each one handed their treasures to the stranger, and as he put them in the pot, each child asked, "Can I have some stone soup now?"

Each time, the stranger looked down into the pot and said, "It's not ready yet."

Of course, the grown-ups in the village noticed all this running around, and they started wandering out of their homes, shading their eyes from the bright sunshine. They followed the children to see what was going on and formed a big circle of grown-ups standing around the smaller circle of children who were sitting around the stranger and the pot.

One man, who had seen his family's last turnip go into the pot, got angry. He stepped up to the stranger and demanded his turnip back. The stranger said, "Go ahead and take it."

The man looked down into the pot, but everything was all bubbly and mixed up, and he couldn't find his turnip, so he turned around and went back to the circle of adults, sad that he would never see that turnip again.

Finally, a tiny little girl stepped to the center of the circle and held out her hand to the stranger. She opened her hand to show a few rocks of dried salt. The stranger smiled at her and took the salt and rubbed it between his hands over the pot. As the crystals of salt hit the bubbling soup, they let out the most delicious smell. Nobody in the village had smelled anything like it for a year.

"Now," said the stranger, "it is ready."

An old lady in the back, who felt sad because she had nothing to bring to the pot, suddenly ran off to her little cabin as fast as her old legs could carry her. She came back with her arms full of bowls and spoons and handed them out. One by one, the people stepped up to the stranger, and he scooped two spoonfuls of hot soup into each bowl.

As the people ate the delicious hot soup, they wandered around and saw neighbors and friends they hadn't seen all year. They laughed with the people who had made it through the winter, and they cried over the ones who didn't. A few of the men began to talk about maybe plowing a field together this year. Some of the women talked about opening the market for a day to sell the things they had been making in their homes. There was talk of opening the school if all went well, just for a week or two. Someone even said something about holding a festival come spring. And there was a sound that hadn't been heard in the village for a long time: laughter.

Then that first brave boy, the one who had walked up to the stranger, looked at all this and decided that he should thank the stranger for bringing the magical stone soup to his village. But when he looked, he found that the fire was neatly put out, the stranger and his pot were gone, and all that was left, sitting on the old tree stump, was the stone. He took that stone and slipped it into his pocket, and many years later he told his grandson the story of stone soup, and he gave him the stone. That boy became a man and he gave the story and the stone to his grandson who gave them to his grandson who gave them to . . . well, me. And now I give them both to you.

As for the stranger, well, he was long gone before anyone went looking for him, down the path to the next little village. But before he got there, he reached down and scooped up another small stone. After all, he might need to make stone soup again.

For other versions see "The Tramp and the Old Woman" in *The Atlantic Treasury of Childhood Stories,* selected and edited by Mary D. Hutchinson Hodgkins (Atlantic Monthly Pr., 1924) or "The Rabbit and the Rock Soup" in *The Animals' Own Story Book: A New Book of Old Folk Tales Chiefly American,* retold by Ellen C. Babbitt (Appleton-Century, 1941).

Aesop's Fables

Aesop's fables are full of short, funny, impacting stories, including many that feature intelligent characters finding their way in a tough world. The best known ones are a part of the very language we speak, from "The Boy Who Cried Wolf" to "The Tortoise and the Hare." There are many lesser-known ones, though, that will appeal to boys, even those in early adolescence. These are great to offer boys who are leaning to tell stories. Be careful of the versions you use. Many have been boiled down to stark cautionary tales, where the fables should be full of mirth and life. Here is how I tell some of my favorites.

Aesop and the Bread Bag

Once, a merchant decided to take all his goods and go to a city two days' travel away to sell them at a market there. He told all his servants to grab a bag to carry on the trip. Now one of the servants was a storyteller, and a very clever man, and he turned to the other servants and said, "Let me choose first which bag to carry, and I will tell you all stories the whole way and make the trip more fun."

The other servants agreed and expected the storyteller to choose the lightest bag. Instead, he chose the biggest, heaviest bag of them all, the bag full of bread for everyone to eat on the trip. Everybody thought he was crazy when he picked the bag up, staggered under its weight, and began walking away.

That first morning was very hard for the storyteller, but when they stopped in the middle of the day, he took bread from his bag and gave each of the other servants a loaf for lunch. When they started out again, the bag was a lot lighter. That night, the troupe stopped again, and the storyteller gave a loaf to each servant for his dinner. The next morning, before they set out, the storyteller gave each servant a loaf for breakfast and his bag was empty. He had nothing to carry all day. But the other servants weren't mad at him because he told such wonderful stories that the trip really was easier for everyone.

The storyteller's name was Aesop, and these are some of his stories.

The Man, the Boy, and the Donkey

An old farmer wanted to sell his donkey at the market, so he set off with his son, leading the donkey by a rope. Some women saw them and laughed, saying, "Why should you walk when you have a donkey carrying nothing at all? One of you should ride."

Well, the old man didn't want people laughing at him, so he lifted the boy up on the donkey to ride. A little later, some old men saw them and were angry.

"Why should you walk, old man, while that good-for-nothing boy rides?"

Well, the old man didn't want people mad at him, so he took the boy off the donkey and climbed up himself to ride.

A little later, some children saw them and were sad.

"Why should a little boy have to walk when a grown man gets to ride?"

Well, the man didn't want anyone sad because of him, so he pulled the boy up and they both rode for a while.

A little later, a farmer saw them and asked where they were going.

"We are going to market to sell this donkey," the man replied.

"Well," the farmer said, "I don't think he will be worth much after carrying you two all day. He looks dead tired already. It would be easier for the two of you to carry him than for him to carry the two of you."

So, wanting to make the farmer happy, the man and the boy got off the donkey and began to carry it on their backs.

Well, the donkey didn't like being carried, and he made a lot of noise. People came from all over to laugh at the silly man and the silly boy trying to carry a donkey. When they got to a bridge, the donkey gave a great kick, splashed into the stream, and was never seen again.

Moral: Trying to please everyone, you might end up pleasing no one.

The Blind Man and the Lame Man

A blind man was trying to get to town, feeling his way with a stick, when his stick hit a patch of mud. He poked all around, but he could not find a way around the mud, so he sat down on a log to think. Along came a lame man, leaning on a cane and moving very slowly. He sat down on the log as well to rest.

"Could you help me?" asked the blind man. "I am blind and I can't see my way through the mud."

"I can't help you much," said the lame man. "I'm lame and can't walk as fast as you can with those strong legs of yours."

The two thought for a second, and then the lame man had an idea.

"My eyes are strong," the lame man said, "and your legs are strong. I will be your eyes if you will be my legs."

So the lame man climbed up on the blind man's shoulders and told him where to put his feet, and the blind man carried the lame man with ease. And soon enough they had gotten to town much faster than they expected.

Moral: Cooperation makes the world a better place.

The Sick Lion and the Fox

The lion found one day that he was getting old, and he feared that the day would come when he could not catch his food and he would starve. So he crawled into his cave and sent word to all the animals of the forest that the lion, their king, was dying, and that all animals should come to say goodbye.

The antelope was the first to heed the call. He came to the mouth of the lion's cave and called out, "Oh mighty king, I, the antelope, have come as you commanded."

The lion called out, "My friend the antelope, please come in where I can see you better, for my eyes are so tired I am nearly blind."

The antelope stepped into the cave and the lion pounced on him and ate him. The next day, the bear arrived. He came to the mouth of the cave and cried out, "Oh mighty king, it is I, the bear, come to say goodbye as you commanded."

The lion called out, "My friend bear? Is that you? Please come closer so I can hear you. I am grown so old and feeble I cannot hear what you say."

So the bear went into the cave and the lion pounced on him and ate him. This continued for many days, and the lion began to think he would never have to hunt again. Then one day, the fox arrived. He stood well back from the mouth of the cave and cried out, "Oh mighty king, it is I, the fox. Did you call for me?"

The lion called out, "Friend fox, dearest of all, come in so that I may give you a gift with my dying breath."

But fox lay down outside the cave and would not come in.

"What is wrong?" called the lion. "Won't you come into my cave?"

"I think not," said the fox, "for I see many footprints leading into your cave, and none coming out."

Moral: Never get into a situation unless you know how you will get out.

The Cats and the Monkey

Two cats found a piece of cheese and took it outside to eat it. But when they split it in two, one of the cats said, "Hey, your piece is bigger!"

The other cat said, "No, they are the same size." And the two cats began to argue. After a while, they decided to let the wise old monkey be the judge. They took their pieces of cheese to the monkey and asked him to decide which piece was bigger.

The monkey took out a scale and put one piece of cheese on each side. He said, "See, this piece here is clearly bigger than the other. I will fix that." Then he took a big bite out of the larger piece and put it back on the scale.

"Oh dear," he said. "Now the other piece is bigger. I will fix that too." And he took a big bite out of the other piece of cheese. But when he put the cheese back on the scale, the first piece was bigger again, so he took another bite out of that.

The two cats watched sadly as the monkey took bite after bite out of their cheese until there were only two tiny pieces left.

"There," said the monkey, "now they are the same size." And the two cats thought they would at least get a taste of the cheese, but the monkey said, "Now I know you two would like to reward me for doing you this service and resolving your argument, so I will take these two small pieces of cheese in payment." And he gobbled up the last two pieces of cheese so that the cats got nothing at all.

Now wouldn't it have been better for the cats if they had just settled their own differences, instead making them into a big argument?

The Frog and the Ox

One day, three baby frogs hopped out of their little pond to go and see the world. They hadn't gone far when they reached the edge of a field and saw an enormous ox. They hopped back home as fast as they could to tell their mother.

"Oh mother, mother!" they cried, "we have seen the largest animal in the whole world."

Well, the mother frog, who had never left the pond in her life, thought she was the largest animal in the whole world. So she sucked in some air, puffed out her belly, and said, "Was he bigger than me?"

"Oh yes," said the little frogs, "he was much bigger than you."

So the mother frog sucked in more air, stuck out her belly even farther, and said, "Was he bigger than I am now?"

"Oh, much, much bigger," cried the little frogs.

So the mother frog puffed herself up even more, bigger than she ever had, and said, "Was he bigger than I am now?"

"Oh," said the little frogs, "you aren't even close!"

So the mother frog puffed herself up until she thought she would burst, and . . . Bang! She did burst.

Moral: Do not try to be something you are not.

The Old Man and His Sons

An old man wanted to hand his farm over to his three sons, but the boys fought so much that he was afraid they couldn't work together. So the old man brought the three boys together and held up a large bundle of sticks tied together with string. He said that whoever could break the bundle of sticks in half would get the whole farm. The father handed the oldest one the bundle of sticks. The son tried and tried, but he couldn't break the bundle. So the father handed the bundle to his second son, but he couldn't break it either. The third son tried and failed as well. Then the father took the bundle back, untied the string, and gave a third of the sticks to each son. The sons broke their small bundles easily. Then the father said he would have to hand the farm over to all three of them together.

Moral: Working together makes you stronger; fighting makes you weaker.

THINKING ABOUT THE POWER OF STORIES

In our efforts to promote books and readings we often forget that a book is an object, a piece of solid material that has little value in and of itself. We forget that the real magic is not in the wood, leather, and glue, but in the words. Going further, even when we honor the words written, we sometimes forget that the power of a piece of literature is not wrapped up in the words that are used, but in the heart and soul that make up the story itself. If we are to help boys through tough transitional times in their emotional development and their scholastic progress, with the hope that they will become readers, we may need to break things down into the basics.

Getting to the core may mean taking the physical act of writing out of the authorship of a story. We can eliminate words altogether and represent a story's most basic plot elements through pictures. Conversely, we can take the visual representation out of a story and make it entirely verbal. We can take out the petrified use of words, in the form of lyrics or memorized lines, and replace them with traditional storytelling techniques. Each of these options is true to the spirit of story, while being sensitive to the different learning styles of boys.

NOTES

1. *Oxford Dictionary of Quotations* (London: Oxford Univ. Pr., 1955), 29.
2. Angela Phillips, *The Trouble with Boys* (New York: Basic Books, 1994), 223.

Chapter 7

Reading, Talking, and Promoting Books

*Reading to kids is to ordinary reading
what jazz is to a string quartet.*

—Sean Wilentz, *Reader's Quotation Book*[1]

Many libraries have found books on tape to be an effective way of serving a population they have never before served very well: working-age men. Libraries have always believed that men read less than women do, and so they were a lost audience. We had them in story hour, and we might get them back when they retire, but in between, men were a nonissue in libraries. Then came books on tape, and men began to appear in libraries again.

What does this tell us? It suggests that even though men read less than women do, for all the reasons we have discussed so far, the ability to appreciate a story is still very much alive. It is only lying dormant. I believe that sparking that appreciation is the necessary first step to turning men, whether preadolescent, adolescent, or adult, back on to reading. When should you start? In truth, we should never stop reading to people, from baby programs to poetry nights for seniors.

READING ALOUD TO CHILDREN

Reading aloud to children is beneficial in many ways, especially for those kids who read less, and often that means boys. Reading to kids sparks a love of story and helps to develop a hunger that only reading can satisfy. Some of the benefits that come from reading, such as better comprehension and increased vocabulary, can be had through listening.[2] Literature-based classrooms are bringing back the practice of reading aloud, but not all children are in these types of classrooms, and the classroom experience is not enough.

How do you go about reading to kids? Take a cue from the recent Harry Potter craze and make it an event. Read the first few chapters of an anticipated new book aloud to a gathering. Start a club for kids who like a series of books and read the first few chapters of each installment as it is released. For readers who have difficulty with language, the first few chapters are hardest until they became familiar with the characters, the setting, and any dialect or colloquialisms. Pick out the funny parts and read them aloud.

Hold read-aloud programs in preparation for big events. Many kids' movies are based on books that are at a higher reading level than most of the intended audience. Start an after-school read-aloud of the book a few weeks before the movie is to be released. Make listening to stories exciting and special. It will remind kids of being read to when they were younger, when reading was a joy instead of a chore.

CHILDREN READING ALOUD

Silent, extended reading is what we all envision for the kids we serve and care for, but we need to see that this model will not work for all children, and certainly not for all boys, until their reading skills have developed. One of the approaches we use to develop these skills is to have children read aloud, usually to an adult or within a group of children about the same age. We seek to make reading a social activity, to encourage reading by having kids read to someone else. However, as much as girls may want to do something *with* someone, boys tend to want to do things *for* other people, to be useful. Here, I think, is where many read-aloud programs go astray for boys. Too often, these programs entail having a boy read to a teacher, a grandparent, or a helpful volunteer who is himself expecting to be the one giving. In such cases, the boy is being taught, and he is not likely to get excited about that.

On the other hand, if a boy is reading to someone who is less capable than he, then the boy is being useful, and if his own skills improve in the process, so much the better. I have been involved in a wonderfully successful initiative with a local school librarian, teaching fourth-grade children to read to second-grade children. Over the course of a few weeks, we two librarians met with the fourth graders and showed them the basics of reading aloud: introducing the title, author and illustrator, speaking clearly, pacing, inflection, choosing a suitable place to read, and much more.

When the big day came, we paired up readers and listeners, usually placing boys with boys and girls with girls. Each fourth grader read a book that he or she had prepared, and then brought the second grader to an ever-growing story circle where we librarians were reading some of our favorites until everybody was done. What did we accomplish? We highlighted reading as a social activity. We encouraged older children to model good reading habits to younger children, an approach that was surely more effective than doing it ourselves. We actually had fourth graders excited about reading. And we played to the best instincts of the children, especially the boys, to feel accomplishment through doing something good for someone who was less capable than they.

Another great way to get children reading aloud comes from Salt Lake City, Utah, and Multnomah County, Oregon, where children read to dogs that are specially trained to sit quietly while they are being read to. The program is named READ (Reading Education Assistance Dogs) and is based on the idea that nonjudgmental listening is encouraging to children who might otherwise be reluctant to read. The presence of an animal is also known to be a calming influence.[3] The presence of properly trained animals is important—this program can not be accomplished with just any pet—but the principle should be inspiring. Let the boys see reading as a tool to make them feel helpful and productive. This is empowerment designed for a boy.

BOOKTALKS

As we start to wrap up this discussion of library services to boys, it is worth remembering the final goal, the endgame as I have put it. We want boys reading. We have talked about being welcoming to boys, promoting programs that bring them into the library, feeding their nature, and developing their language skills. All this goes for naught if we cannot put books in their hands. To put it in terms from the fantasy genre, we can be their guides to the very brink, but the final stage of the journey is their own. Now it is time to hand them the book.

Choosing Books to Booktalk

Booktalking is a cherished skill in the library profession, particularly in children's services, but it is also a service that must meet the needs of boys. How does traditional booktalking fail boys? Often by the very selection of books we choose to talk about. When many librarians choose titles to booktalk, whether formally or informally, they choose what they consider the best books. The theory is that kids read little enough, so we should push them to make the most of their reading. As we have seen, librarians often consider the best books to be books that appeal the most to girls. Even when they consciously choose books with male characters or in male genres, they choose the ones that appeal to their own sensibilities. *Johnny Tremain* has a male protagonist, and it is about a boy becoming a man in a time of war, but it is too dated and too focused on domestic relations to be appealing to many of today's adolescent and preadolescent boys.

Following are some practical suggestions for tailoring booktalks for boy appeal and examples of my favorite booktalks. There are many books full of booktalks out there, but they get dated quickly, and boys like to have their books new and fresh. Also, most of the booktalks available are not written with the particular needs of boys in mind. The examples given here are mostly from more recent books, and they are designed specifically to appeal to boys.

We need to be willing to booktalk the books that boys will be drawn to rather than the books we as educators feel are best. That means fantasy, nonfiction, and humor; it may mean books that are action-packed, gross, or even edgy. One of the greatest impromptu booktalks I ever saw came from Stacy DeBole, young adult librarian at the Parlin Library in Everett, Massachusetts. She walked in to a group of adolescents and said, "This book really sucks." Then she slapped the book she was holding against the wall, and the book stuck!

The book, of course, was *This Book Really Sucks! The Science behind Gravity, Flight, Leeches, Black Holes, Tornadoes, Our Friend the Vacuum Cleaner, and Most Everything Else That Sucks* (Planet Dexter, 1999), and the book was covered in tiny suction cups. The booktalk was active, impacting, edgy, and short. The book was nonfiction; the setting was relaxed. A little humor put the librarian in a more human light than we usually enjoy. And guess what? One of the kids took the book to read.

Different Approaches for Boys

When we booktalk, librarians often zero in on the characters in the book and their interpersonal relations. Most children's librarians are women, and this is what we, as a group, feel is most important and interesting about books. We also tend to make booktalks very long and intricate, as if we can reveal all that is great about an entire book in a single discussion. We need to explore different styles of booktalks so we can reach a broad audience. In addition, if we want to reach boys, it is a good idea to keep the booktalks short. Girls are more likely to be drawn in by an emotional setup; boys are looking for the impact. Here are some approaches to booktalking that will appeal specifically to boys, along with illustrative examples of my favorite booktalks.

FIND THE HUMOR

Rather than always focusing on setting up the conflict between characters, or the conflict within a character's mind, focus some of your booktalks on other aspects of the book. Find the humor, and present it quickly and unadorned:

Jon Scieszka. *Summer Reading Is Killing Me* (Viking, 1998)
> As if the title wasn't enough, Winnie-the-Pooh gets carried off by Dracula, and the librarian is really the devil.

Stop there. You do not have to set up the whole book. Besides, there is a boy in the back with his hand up, asking for the book already. Here are a few other favorites:

David Elliott. *The Transmogrification of Roscoe Wizzle* (Candlewick, 2001)
> Transmogrify: "To change or transform, especially into something funny or comical." You know, like when children eat too many hamburgers and turn into bugs. (p. 28)

Richard Jennings. *The Great Whale of Kansas* (Houghton Mifflin, 2001)
> "I was well on my way to having what I've always wanted," I told him. "A pond of my very own. But now there's the possibility of getting something I never even thought of having before, I find that I want it, instead. Is this wrong?" (pp. 19–20)
> Phil said nothing, which is his customary response (since, of course, Phil is a duck).

GETTING A RESPONSE

Use a booktalk to ask questions, and then actually listen to the answers. Get the kids to throw out their own opinions, but don't tell them the answer that is in the book. Boys love to try to assert even with limited knowledge or chance of success. Make them read the book to see if they are right.

Bruce Coville. *Aliens Ate My Homework* (Minstrel, 1993)

> Rod Allbright has three problems: (1) The schoolyard bully keeps smashing bugs in his hair. (2) The most wanted criminal in the entire galaxy is hiding somewhere in his neighborhood. (3) Five aliens hiding in his room just ate a hole in his science fair project. Which one do you think he should take care of first?

Chris Lynch. *Gold Dust* (HarperCollins, 2000)

> Jim Rice and Fred Lynn came to the Red Sox together as rookies in 1975, but Napoleon Charlie Ellis noticed they were not treated quite the same by the Fenway fans, so he turned to his friend Richard and said, "They clap for Fred Lynn even when he appears to have done something foolish."
>
> Richard replies, "They were applauding the effort, Napoleon, the hustle."
>
> "And when he struck out, that took great effort?"
>
> "Maybe."
>
> "He struck out, the same as Jim Rice."
>
> "Like I told you, it happens—"
>
> "But the people clapped madly for Mr. Lynn anyway. Not so much for Mr. Rice. What does that mean Richard?" (pp. 184–85)
>
> So I ask you, what do you suppose made Fred Lynn so different from Jim Rice? Richard knows; he just doesn't want to think about it. Napoleon has to think about it because he's different too.

Then turn the cover so the kids can see. Napoleon, like Jim Rice, is black, and Richard is white. The more guesses the kids make, and the more discussion that follows, the more you might draw the boys into this excellent book which deals with tough social issues, but never skimps on the great baseball action.

Gary Paulsen. *The Car* (Harcourt Brace & Company, 1994)

> Terry is fourteen when his parents have a huge fight. Each one storms out, assuming the other will stay and take care of Terry. They aren't coming back. Now Terry has a house, a put-together roadster in the garage, and a choice. Stay or go? What would you do?

Laurie Myers. *Surviving Brick Johnson* (Clarion, 2000)

> Alex carries baseball cards to help him through his day. They inspire him. If he wants to be fast, he carries the card of a fast player, like Barry Bonds. If he wants to be alert, he carries the catcher, Mike Piazza. Now Brick Johnson is out to maim him; he needs a very special card, one that will inspire him to greatness. Who would you choose?

By the way, Alex wants Ted Williams, but you do not have to tell them that. Here is how you can use this technique to sell a classic to older boys:

Daniel Defoe. *Robinson Crusoe* [Great Illustrated Classics ed.] (Abdo & Daughters, 2002)

> Your ship is wrecked, killing all your companions. Is God punishing you? You alone survive. Is God protecting you? Twenty years marooned on an island you thought was deserted, but now you discover you are not alone. Do you want to know who is waiting for you on the other side of the island? Ask Robinson Crusoe.

APPEAL TO REASON

Appeal to boys' logical approach—their desire to put things in categories and make them understandable. Lists, categorization, and structure speak to boys looking for these things in an unsure world.

Ken Roberts. *The Thumb in the Box* (Douglas & McIntyre, 2001)

> The little village of New Aukland, Canada, has one girl who knows everything, one boy who can't stop smiling, one fire truck stuck in the mud, no roads, one African lion, a severe shortage of playground equipment, one world-famous painter, and a man who can take off his thumb and put it in a box. Find out what it all means in *A Thumb in the Box*.

Richard Jennings. *The Great Whale of Kansas* (Houghton Mifflin, 2001)

> "Facts are funny things. No matter how many you discover, there are always more you know you should have found. . . . On any given day, the facts we know can be replaced by those we don't. Honestly, it wouldn't surprise me if after we're dead, we found out we didn't know anything at all." Fact: Melville, Kansas, is the geographic center of the United States. Fact: Higly Park, in Melville, Kansas, is a very quiet place. Fact: There were no whales in the age of dinosaurs. Two of these three facts are about to change in *The Great Whale of Kansas*.

You can even use the logical approach to confound by setting up an illogical twist, creating tension and interest. Promote this book that boys will find comforting and familiar, if you can only get past its childish reputation, by appealing to, and then turning on its head, a little logical development.

A. A. Milne. *The House at Pooh Corner* (Puffin, 1992)

"Rabbit is clever," said Pooh thoughtfully.

"Yes," said Piglet, "Rabbit is clever."

"And he has Brain."

"Yes," said Piglet, "Rabbit has Brain."

"I suppose," said Pooh, "that that's why he never understands anything." (p. 131)

Here is another example of a logical twist:

David Elliott. *The Transmogrification of Roscoe Wizzle* (Candlewick, 2001)

"I used to be a normal kid. I mean, don't get me wrong, I still am normal. But once you get changed into a bug, you do see things a little bit differently. . . ." (p. 8) So says Roscoe Wizzle in *The Transmogrification of Roscoe Wizzle*.

GUILTY PLEASURES

Highlight the ways in which a book is wrong or bad. Most boys think most books are written for girls, so tell them why this book is different. Boys love books that give them a guilty pleasure, so use that as your hook. Tell them all about the things they are not supposed to enjoy. Say this first one with an increasingly snotty voice:

Lemony Snicket. A Series of Unfortunate Events. *The Bad Beginning* (HarperCollins, 1999)

Don't you just hate happy endings? Don't you just hate it when the bad guy always loses? Don't you just hate stories about perfect little children living with their perfect little parents in a perfect little town in their perfect little house with their perfect little dog? Well if you do, then you may be one of the special few to enjoy A Series of Unfortunate Events. In book one alone, three perfect children run into a disastrous fire, a mean and greedy count, ugly clothing, and cold oatmeal for breakfast. And it only gets worse!

Boys' humor is generally frowned upon. Mention of bodily functions or body parts, silly puns, and good-natured ribbing are things we adults do not encourage. Tell a boy such things are in a book and they are likely to leap out of their seats to get it.

Jon Scieszka. The Time Warp Trio. *Sam Samurai* (Viking, 2001)

    The Samurai scowled down at us. "No one disturbs our master's peace with their entertainments unless they ask me, leader of the Red Devil bodyguards, Owattabutt." The samurai posed proudly.

    Fred's eyes bugged out. I couldn't stop him.

    "Oh what a butt?" asked Fred.

    "Owattabutt of Minowa," said the samurai.

    "Oh—what a butt," repeated Sam.

    We tried our best not to laugh. We really did. But you know us.

    It took us about three seconds to crack up, freak out Owattabutt, have our hands tied behind our backs, and get surrounded by a gang of red samurai warriors with spears.

    Then things really went bad. (p. 55)

    How could they get worse? Read *Sam Samurai* by Jon Scieszka and find out.

    Look for, and point out, scary parts and gross scenes. Leave something to the imagination, though:

Laurie Myers. *Surviving Brick Johnson* (Clarion, 2000)

    Alex thinks that Brick Johnson, the biggest kid in school, is going to maim him. The only problem is, he doesn't know what "maim" means, so he looks it up in the dictionary.

    "maim. 1. to cause serious physical injury."

    Yep. That made sense. Brick did want to cause him serious physical injury. The second and third definitions were worse.

    "maim. 2. to disable or make defective."

    "maim. 3. to deprive a person of a limb or member of the body."

    "Mom, exactly how important are the second and third definitions of a word?"

    "It depends on the word." (pp. 6–7)

    That was the answer Alex hated most. It depends. Brick would know all the possible definitions for maim. . . . Maybe Brick was planning all three!

Lemony Snicket. A Series of Unfortunate Events. *Reptile Room*
(HarperCollins, 1999)

With a flourish he swooped the cloth off the cage. Inside was a large
black snake, as dark as a coal mine and as thick as a sewer pipe, looking
right at the orphans with shiny green eyes. With the cloth off its cage, the
snake began to uncoil itself and slither around his home.

"What's it called?" Violet asked.

"The Incredibly Deadly Viper," Uncle Monte replied, and at that
moment something happened which I'm sure will interest you. With one
flick of its tail, the snake unlatched the door of its cage and slithered out
onto the table, and before Uncle Monty or any of the Baudelaire orphans
could say anything, it opened its mouth and . . .

[Stop here and wait for loud objections. If you get enough of them,
finish the sentence.]

. . . before Uncle Monty or any of the Baudelaire orphans could say
anything, it opened its mouth and bit Sunny right on the chin. (p. 26)

To find out what happens next, you will have to read *The Reptile
Room* by Lemony Snicket.

ISSUE A CHALLENGE

Challenge boys. Tell them they cannot handle a book—that it is too gross, too
weird, even too funny. This example is a picture book with a good amount of
text and vocabulary that is challenging but interesting. It is a nice read for a
third grader struggling with language.

Mary Elise Monsell. Pictures by Lynn Munsinger. *Underwear!* (Whitman,
1988)

[Hide the book behind your back.] I have the funniest book ever written
in my hand. This book is so hilariously funny that children older than
you have been known to turn purple and pass out just looking at the pictures. Scientists at NASA have failed to adequately explain how this book
got to be just this funny. No living human being has ever been able to
read this book, out loud, without laughing so hard their spleen burst.
Sadly, tragically, thousands have tried and paid the price. Are you ready
for the challenge? Can you do it without laughing? Do you dare read . . .
Underwear!?

If someone wants to try, go ahead and let them. Which is more important, your schedule or one child's chance to succeed at reading? This one is a

little more serious, and the book is aimed at the higher end of the age group we are dealing with:

Darren Shan. *Cirque Du Freak* (Little, Brown, 2001)

If you get frightened easily by creepy crawly things, feel free to cover your ears while I talk about this next book. If you like that sort of thing, try to picture the following scene vividly in your mind:

I don't know if Mr. Crepsley was really scared, or if it was part of the act, but he looked frightened. He wiped the sleeve of his right arm over his forehead, then placed the flute back in his mouth and whistled a strange little tune.

Madam Octa cocked her head, then appeared to nod. She crawled across the table until she was in front of Mr. Crepsley. He lowered his right hand and she crept up his arm. The thought of those long hairy legs creeping along his flesh made me sweat all over. And I liked spiders! People who were afraid of them must have been nervously chewing the insides of their cheeks to pieces.

When she got to the top of his arm, she scuttled along his shoulder, up his neck, over his ear, and didn't stop until she reached the top of his head, where she lowered her body. She looked like a funny kind of hat. After a while, Mr. Crepsley began playing the flute again. Madam Octa slid down the other side of his face, along the scar, and walked around until she was standing upside down on his chin. Then she spun a string of web and dropped down on it.

She was hanging about three inches below his chin now, and slowly began rocking from side to side. Soon she was swinging about level with his ears. Her legs were tucked in, and from where I was sitting she looked like a ball of wool.

Then, as she made an upward swing, Mr. Crepsley threw his head back and she went flying up into mid air. . . . I thought she'd land on the floor or the table, but she didn't. Instead, she landed in Mr. Crepsley's mouth! (pp. 80–81)

And that's just one of the acts in the *Cirque Du Freak!*

Mysteries, of course, are great for a challenge. Give out one clue at a time and let the children guess the outcome. Of course they will not be able to, or at least they will not know for sure, but if they have already been drawn in by the challenge of solving the mystery, then they are more likely to want to read the book.

Bruce Hale. *The Big Nap: A Chet Gecko Mystery* (Harcourt, 2001)

> Something was very wrong at Emerson Hicky Elementary school. What could make otherwise normal, wisecracking goof-offs clean blackboards, study during recess, and actually pay attention during science class? I mean, this was weird. Everywhere, students were walking stiff-legged and slow, with a dazed look in their eyes, saying things like "School good" and "Must study" and "Must help teacher. Teacher good." Who could be behind it? Could it be the furry kid in the magician's hat practicing hypnosis? The smooth talking new weasel in town? Or could it be that really big new librarian with the dark glasses, a funny way of talking, and all the books on zombies? Whoever it is, they better watch out, because for seventy-five cents and all the mosquito milk shakes he can drink, Chet Gecko, private eye, is on the case.

Peter Lerangis. Abracadabra. *Poof! Rabbits Everywhere* (Scholastic, 2001)

> When a rabbit pops up in school out of nowhere, it's pretty funny. When three show up, it's distracting. When five show up, it's annoying. When seven show up, the principal of Rebus Elementary School threatens to kick the Abracadabra Club out of school unless they can prove they really aren't pulling these rabbits out of their hats. Maybe the person to blame is the suspicious looking man from the magic shop who has been putting on disguises and hanging around school, but they better find some proof soon or it is the Magic Club that will disappear.

ACTION

Do not forget the sports books. Many provide great action scenes and wonderful opportunities for cliffhangers, and kids playing sports are an immediate connection for young male readers:

Gordon Korman. *The Chicken Doesn't Skate* (Scholastic, 1996)

> What is a chicken? Some say it is a pet, others see it as a meal with feathers, still others see it as a wondrous work of nature, but there are some who believe a chicken is really the secret weapon of the South Middle School Rangers hockey team! How can a chicken win a hockey championship? Find out in *The Chicken Doesn't Skate* by Gordon Korman.

Chris Lynch. *Gold Dust* (HarperCollins, 2000)

> I stand in there, scratching hard into the frozen dirt of the petrified batter's box with my spikes. Butchie keeps grinning, leans back, and back and back, then comes over the top, and over and over, and finally reaches his perfect release point and lets go of the first pitch of the 1975 baseball season.

It whistles. It is such a beautiful thing, the sound of it, the East-West spin—which I can pick up easily in the superior clarity of winter's air—that I am almost too excited to react properly to the pitch until . . .

I drop to the ground, flopping hard on my back an instant before the ball nails me in the head.

"If you can't stand the heat . . ." Butchie says, blowing warm steaming air through his pitching hand.

Could've told you he was going to do that.

I do love this game. (pp. 8–9)

The same approach works for action and adventure. Remember what draws boys to these types of books and focus in on the danger, the challenge, and the wide open spaces:

Sid Hite. *Stick & Whittle* (Scholastic, 2000)

What are the chances that two guys named Melvin would run into each other in the vast open plains of Indian country? What are the chances that a soldier that has been gone for eight years could find his long lost sweetheart when all he knows is that she is somewhere out West? And what are the chances that a dead man, two teenagers, and one old Indian could rescue the captives from a band of well-armed desperados in a heavily fortified canyon? Well, when Stick and Whittle are involved, anything is possible.

TAKE THEM ON A JOURNEY

When you present fantasy, be mindful of the aspects that appeal to boys, as opposed to the ones that appeal to librarians. Represent the journey, the quest, and the cosmic battles of good and evil rather than the personal struggles and everyday details of the characters' lives. Draw the boys into the other world that exists in all fantasy:

Emily Drake. *The Magickers* (Daw, 2001)

Camp Ravenwyng is just like any other summer camp. It has cabins, counselors, a lake, arts and crafts, and campfires. Of course, one of the cabins is haunted, one of the counselors hovers a foot above the ground, the lake has a sea monster, arts and crafts includes learning how to use magic crystals, and the campfires are held under the gathering clouds of a magical storm that could signal the end of the world as we know it.

Checklist: Booktalking Points to Remember

When preparing booktalks with boys in mind, remember:

Keep it short.

Find the humor.

Ask questions and listen to answers.

Appeal to boys' logical approach.

Offer a guilty pleasure.

Challenge them.

Let them try to guess the ending.

Highlight the action and suspense in sports and adventure books.

Bring out the quest, the journey, and the battle between good
and evil in fantasy.

THOUGHTS ON TALKING BOOKS

Talk about books. Read books aloud. Add your voice to the cause. Do you know why librarians are considered passive and retiring? Because all too often we are. If getting kids, especially boys, to read is that important to us, then we need to speak up. While we need to speak about the importance of books and reading on special occasions and in front of large audiences, it is the day-to-day opportunities to talk about books that will ultimately have the greatest impact. Talk about books in your programs. Go into classrooms and talk about books. Carry a book around the library some afternoon and tell everyone you cannot put it down until you convince someone to read it. Realize that boys need books just as much as girls do, and girls are more likely to read than boys are, so use that as motivation. Seeing kids read is the validation of all that we do.

NOTES

1. *Reader's Quotation Book* (Wainscott, N.Y.: Pushcart, 1990), 142.
2. Stephen Krashen, *The Power of Reading: Insights from the Research* (Englewood, Colo.: Libraries Unlimited, 1993), 39–44.
3. Susan G. Hauser, "Reading? It's for the Dogs," *Wall Street Journal* (August 9, 2001): A.10.

CONCLUSION

Across the fields of yesterday
He sometimes comes to me,
A little lad just back from play—
The lad I used to be.

—T. S. Jones Jr.,
"Sometimes," *Pocket Book of Quotations*[1]

In the end, we want boys to read. It is such a simple goal, but obviously we find ourselves challenged, frustrated, even thwarted by it. Much works against our success. Boys must overcome challenges from within and obstructions from without to become active readers.

External forces push in on boys, making it harder for them to develop as readers. Peer pressure, social stereotypes, and an aggressive mass media bombard the preadolescent boy with discouragements. Men are active, assertive, heedless of consequences, and disparaging of mental activity. Reinforcing these images, boys do not see men read. The people they see in schools and libraries are almost exclusively women.

At the same time, boys face challenges to their becoming readers from within. Boys themselves are active creatures. They are driven by utilitarian concerns. Their wish is to understand the world around them. Their impulse is to take to their heels and go. If something is worth knowing, then it is worth experiencing in person. They see reading as passive, reflective, and girlish.

This leaves boys at a disadvantage in our modern world. Without an active reading life, boys are almost destined to fall behind, and stay behind, in the acquisition and effective use of language. Their ability to pick up new skills and consider new ideas will be irreparably impaired. At the very least, they will miss out, for a lifetime, on the pure joy of losing oneself in a book. At worst, they will be doomed to go only as far as their muscles can carry them.

This gloomy picture does not have to be. Librarians have the weapon we need to battle aliteracy. We have programming. Programs have long been the tool librarians use to reach out to people, to bring them into our libraries, and to encourage them to read. Unfortunately, our programs have often favored the needs and interests of girls and women over those of boys and men.

To correct this oversight, we must develop programs that recognize the difference between the male and the female views of reading. The first step may well be recognizing that we, as a profession, are predominantly female, and our first thoughts may betray a particularly female point of view. This challenge is not insurmountable because we are not subject to strict determinism. Our first thoughts may betray a bias, but we are rational, flexible, and, as a profession, wholly committed to equality of service. We simply need to apply some basic understanding of the way boys operate.

We must welcome challenge and competition into our libraries. If we view competitiveness as a social evil, then we will project to every boy who crosses our paths that a basic component of his psyche is wrong, so he himself is flawed. If we welcome competition, even integrate it into our programs, boys will feel comfortable, even excited, around books and reading. If we tie reading to competitive activities, then we will intertwine reading into activities that boys love.

We must be accepting of active learning and of active boys. We can show boys that they are welcome by building programs with a physical component. We can recognize that boys' minds are engaged when their hands are employed. We need to acknowledge that rules mandating silent, solitary, sedentary conduct all but exclude preadolescent boys. They are also random, based more on past practice than necessity.

We must honor reading preferences that are in conflict with our own. We have to recognize that the books deemed best for libraries and for children's collections are so designated because of a particularly feminine point of view. When honoring themes and genres, we prefer interpersonal connections and internal struggles, but these do not speak to boys the way they speak to girls. Boys prefer the external struggle and the heroic quest. Fantasy, sports, and the epic journey are all routes to the heart and mind of a boy.

We must see that boys have developmental issues that make reading a chore and language an obstacle. Boys develop later, on average, than girls do.

Boys' reading skills suffer as they struggle with other transitional issues, issues of identity, separation, and social development, in the early elementary years. We need to realize that these transitional issues can put boys so far behind in reading they may never catch up. We can help boys through this struggle by offering recreational reading that they can identify with, and by allowing them to read below their level if that is what it takes to develop good reading habits.

We must recognize that boys long for role models, and that their world is largely devoid of men. If we fail to give boys male role models who read, then they are likely to find their own role models with more destructive habits. We need to be welcoming and encouraging to men, to bring men from the community into the library, in order to defeat the perception that libraries are feminine enclaves, and that reading is for girls.

We can accomplish these objectives by applying the best of traditional librarianship and being open to new ways of doing things. In the end, our libraries may look very different than they have in the past, and if one of the differences is a more equal presence for men and boys, then we will know that we have done well, and a new generation may wonder why boys were ever hard to find in the library.

NOTE

1. *Pocket Book of Quotations* (New York: Pocket Books, 1952), 21.

BIBLIOGRAPHY

Abilock, Debbie. "Sex in the Library: How Gender Differences Should Affect Practices and Programs." *Emergency Librarian* (May/June 1997): 17–18.

American Library Association. Access to Library Resources and Services regardless of Gender or Sexual Orientation, 2000, available at http://www.ala.org/alaorg/oif/acc_gend.html/. Accessed July 22, 2002.

Aronson, Marc. *Exploding the Myths: The Truth about Teenagers and Reading.* Lantham, Md.: Scarecrow, 2001.

Ashby, Susan. "Reading Doesn't Have to Damage Your Street Cred." *Youth Studies Australia* 17 (March 1998): 46.

Battle of the Books: Voluntary Reading Incentive Program, available at http://www.battleofthebooks.org/. Accessed August 12, 2002.

Beales, Donna. *Knights of the Ring: How to Build an Enthusiastic Junior Friends of the Library Group in Six Weeks . . . and Make It Last.* Lowell, Mass.: DLB, 1997.

———. "Lords of the Library." *School Library Journal* 43 (May 1997): 65.

"Bits & Pieces." *Library Imagination Paper* 20 (winter 1998): 4.

Boy Scout Requirements, 2002. Irving, Tex.: Boy Scouts of America, 2002.

Butler, Janet. "Making Reading a 'Guy Thing.'" *Reading Today* 18 (June/July 2001): 20.

Cart, Michael. "What about Boys?" *Booklist* 96 (January 1, 2000 & January 15, 2000): 892.

"Chess Kings: Harlem Kids Score in a Classic Game of Strategy." *Time for Kids* 5 (January 28, 2000): 7.

Clark, Beverly Lyon, and Margaret R. Higonnet, eds. *Girls, Boys, Books, Toys: Gender in Children's Literature and Culture.* Baltimore: Johns Hopkins Univ. Pr., 1999.

Crawford, Walt, and Michael Gorman. *Future Libraries: Dreams, Madness, and Reality.* Chicago: American Library Assn., 1995.

Crittenden, Danielle. "Boy Meets Book." *Wall Street Journal—Eastern Edition* 234 (November 26, 1999): 13.

Cub Scout Tiger Cub Handbook. Irving, Tex.: Boy Scouts of America, 2001.

Dobrez, Cindy, and Lynn Rutan. "Mapping March Madness: Here's a Sneaky Way to Lure Kids (Especially Boys) into the Library." *School Library Journal* 48 (February 2002): 43.

Fulghum, Robert. *It Was on Fire When I Lay Down on It.* New York: Villard, 1989.

Hartlage-Striby, Karen. "Girls Choose Fiction; Boys Choose Non-Fiction." *Kentucky Libraries* 65 (fall 2001): 36–39.

Hauser, Susan G. "Reading? It's for the Dogs." *Wall Street Journal* (August 9, 2001): A.10.

Hawley, David. "In Minneapolis, Chess Spectators Can't Keep Tempers in Check." *Saint Paul Pioneer Press* (May 18, 2001): 1.

"How to . . . Keep Boys Interested in Books." *NEA Today* 19 (January 2001): 27.

Kaplan, Paul. "The Boys and Girls of Summer: Baseball Theme Programming Tips to Catch Young Readers." *Illinois Libraries* 81 (fall 1999): 214–17.

Katusic, Slavica K., Robert C. Colligan, William J. Barbaresi, et al. "Incidence of Reading Disability in a Population-Based Birth Cohort, 1976–1982, Rochester, Minn." *Mayo Clinic Proceedings* 76 (2001): 1081–92.

"Kingmakers: Young Players Flock to Chess at a Time When Its Academic Benefits Draw Notice." *Christian Science Monitor* 91 (August 10, 1999): 15.

Krashen, Stephen. *The Power of Reading: Insights from the Research.* Englewood, Colo.: Libraries Unlimited, 1993.

Lamm, Bob. "Reading Groups: Where Are All the Men?" *Publishers Weekly* 243 (November 18, 1996): 48.

Landsberg, Michelle. *Reading for the Love of It: Best Books for Young Readers.* New York: Prentice-Hall, 1987.

Langerman, Deborah. "Books and Boys: Gender Preferences and Book Selection." *School Library Journal* 36 (March 1990): 132–36.

Lipson, Eden Ross. "Books' Hero Wins Young Minds." *New York Times,* July 7, 1999, p.1.

Love, Kristina, and Julie Hamston. "Out of the Mouths of Boys: A Profile of Boys Committed to Reading." *Australian Journal of Language and Literacy* 24 (February 2001): 31+.

Lypsyte, Robert. "Listening for the Footsteps: Books and Boys." *The Horn Book* 68 (May/June 1992) 290–96.

Marvel, Mark. "Reading the Male." *Esquire* 126 (December 1996): 40.

Moloney, James. "Books to Put in a Boy's Hand." *Magpies* 15 (November 2000): 10–12.

———. "We Don't Read Because We Want to Be Men." *Magpies* 14 (March 1999): 10–14.

Murphy, Jendy. "Boys Will Be Boys: A Public Librarian Leads Her First Book Group for the Opposite Sex." *School Library Journal* 47 (January 2001): 31.

Newmann, Sandford A., James Alan Fox, Edward A. Flynn, et al. *America's After-School Choice: The Prime Time for Juvenile Crime, or Youth Enrichment and Achievement.* Washington, D.C.: Fight Crime: Invest in Kids, 2000.

Nicolle, Ray. "Boys and the Five-Year Void." *School Library Journal* 35 (March 1989): 130.

Nielsen, Alleen Pace. "It's Deja Vu All Over Again!" *School Library Journal* 47 (March 2001): 49–50.

OCL Summer Reading Program 2001, available at http://www.ocl.net/sleuth/. Accessed August 12, 2002.

Odean, Kathleen. *Great Books for Boys.* New York: Ballantine, 1998.

Oxford Dictionary of Quotations. London: Oxford Univ. Pr., 1955.

Phillips, Angela. *The Trouble with Boys.* New York: Basic Books, 1994.

Piper, Paul S., and Barbara E. Collamer. "Male Librarians: Men in a Feminized Profession." *Journal of Academic Librarianship* 27 (September 2001): 406–11.

Plesser, Francine. "Programs with Boys and Girls Together." *VOYA* 18 (April 1995): 11–12.

Pocket Book of Quotations. New York: Pocket Books, 1952.

Pollack, William. *Real Boys' Voices.* New York: Random House, 2000.

Read Across America, available at http://www.nea.org/readacross/. Accessed July 30, 2002.

Reader's Quotation Book. Wainscott, N.Y.: Pushcart, 1990.

Rehard, Karen. "Books for Boys." *Book Links* 4 (May 1995) 45–50.

Renwick, Lucille. "What's the Buzz?" *Instructor* 111 (August 2001): 8.

Richardson, Jean L., Barbara Radziszewska, Clyde W. Dent, et al. "Relationship between After-School Care of Adolescents and Substance Use, Risk Taking, Depressed Mood, and Academic Achievement." *Pediatrics* 92 (July 1993): 32–38.

Saskatchewan Library Association Summer Reading Program, available at http://www.lib.sk.ca/sla/srp.htm/. Accessed August 12, 2002.

Scieszka, Jon. "Guys Read," at www.guysread.com.

Sommers, Christina Hoff. *The War against Boys.* New York: Simon & Schuster, 2000.

Steiner, Stanley F. "Where Have All the Men Gone? Male Role Models in the Reading Crisis." *PNLA Quarterly* 64 (summer 2000): 17.

"Study Finds Boys More Likely to Have Reading Disabilities." *ASHA Leader* 6 (December 11, 2001): 3.

Summer Reading Program Packets Available at Wyoming State Library, available at http://www-wsl.state.wy.us/slpub/summer_reading.html#S/. Accessed August 12, 2002.

Witt, Peter, and Dwayne Baker, "Developing After-School Programs for Youth in High Risk Environments." *Journal of Physical Education, Recreation & Dance* 69 (November/December 1997): 18.

Wolf Cub Scout Book. Irving, Tex.: Boy Scouts of America, 2001.

Wyckoff, Malia McCawley. "Beyond Harry Potter: The Books Boys Can't Resist Reading." *Family Life* (October 2000): 86.

INDEX

A

Abilock, Debbie, 14
Abuse. *See* Safety issues
Acquisition of books. *See also* Resources
    discouragement of reading and, 27–29
    respect for boys' choices and, 27
"Aesop and the Bread Bag," 88–89
Aesop's fables
    "Aesop and the Bread Bag," 88–89
    "Blind Man and the Lame Man," 90
    "Cats and the Monkey," 91–92
    "Frog and the Ox," 92–93
    "Man, the Boy, and the Donkey," 89–90
    "Old Man and His Sons," 93
    "Sick Lion and the Fox," 91
Alexander, Lloyd, 26
Aliens Ate My Homework, 100
Aliteracy, 57, 110
America's Battle of the Books, 67
Anansi the spider, 81
*Animals' Own Story Book: A New Book of Old
    Folk Tales Chiefly American*, 88
Aronson, Marc, 29
Art
    incorporation of, 36
    use of crafts, 49–50
    visual storytelling and, 74
Atlantic Treasury of Childhood Stories, 88

B

Babbitt, Ellen C., 88
Background checks, 16–17, 20
Bad Beginning, 102
Battle of the Books, 67

Beales, Donna, 32
Behavior
    boys in libraries and, 10, 12–15, 70–71
    challenging boys, 15
Big Nap: A Chet Gecko Mystery, 106
Biographies, 25
"Blind Man and the Lame Man," 90
Book discussion groups, 34–37
Book of Lost Tales, 34
Booktalks
    appeal to reason approach for, 101–2
    challenge approach for, 104–6
    fantasy approach for, 107
    guilty pleasure approach for, 102–4
    humorous approach for, 99
    sports/action approach for, 106–7
Boy Scouts, 46–47, 55–56
Bradley, Marion Zimmer, 26

C

Car, 100
"Cats and the Monkey," 91–92
Celtic Magic Tales, 84
Challenges for boys, 15, 104–5
Checkers, 66
Chess
    banned in libraries, 70–71
    Parlin Library Chess Program, 59–60
    planning/initiating library program for,
        60–62
    tournaments, 63–64
    variations of, 64–66
Chicken Doesn't Skate, 106
Cirque Du Freak, 105

Collaborative efforts. *See* School-library connections

Communication, 3, 109–10

Communities
   library programming and, xiii
   non-parents volunteering in, 17–18
   Read Across America and, 50

Competition, xiii-xiv, 104–6, 110. *See also* Chess

Coville, Bruce, 100

Crafts, 49

Cub Scouts, 46–47

"Cuchulainn and the King of the Fairy Folk," 81–84

D

Defoe, Daniel, 101

Demographics and library attendance after school, 11

Dinosaur!, 74

Discrimination and boys' behavior, 6, 10, 13, 70–71

Discussion groups. *See* Book discussion groups

Displays, 31

Dobrez, Cindy, 30

Dr. Seuss, 49–51

Drake, Emily, 107

Dungeons and Dragons, 32

E

Elliott, David, 99, 102

Ethics, 6

Evaluations of cooperative efforts, 52

Exploding the Myths: The Truth about Teenagers and Reading, 29

F

Fantasy
   competitive role-playing and, 66–67
   promotion of reading and, 25–27, 32–34
   resources for, 38–40, 107

Field trips, 51–52

Folktales, 80–81. *See also* Aesop's fables; Storytelling

Food in the library, 12

"Frog and the Ox," 92–93

G

Games. *See also* Storytelling
   banned in libraries, 70–71
   board games/role playing, 66–67
   chess, 59–66
   homeschooled children and, 69–70

Gender roles
   aliteracy and, 57
   boys' behavior and, 12–13, 68
   chess and, 58, 66
   choosing stories for boys and, 80–81
   competitive mystery programs and, 67–68
   discouragement of reading and, 27–29
   external forces and, 109–11
   genres of reading for boys and, 22–25
   stereotypes and, 58
   storytelling and, 73–74

Genres
   boys' choices, 22–27
   fantasy/medieval, 25–27, 32–34, 38–40, 66–67, 107
   mystery/suspense, 42, 67–68, 105–6
   science fiction, 40–41
   sports/outdoors, 24–25, 29–32, 38, 106–7

Geography, 49

Gold Dust, 100, 106–7

Grammar skills, 42

Great Whale of Kansas, 99, 101

Group work, 13–14

Guest speakers, 30

H

Hale, Bruce, 106

Harry Potter series, 32, 34, 67

High King, 27

Hite, Sid, 107

Hobbit, 34

Hodgkins, Mary D. Hutchinson, 88

Homeschooled children, 69–70

House at Pooh Corner, 102

How to Eat Fried Worms, 24

Humor
   as boys' choice, 24, 26
   guilty pleasure and, 102–3
   resources for, 41
   use of, 11–12

I

Illinois Librarians, 29
Illustrations, 74
Irish Folklore, 84

J

Jennings, Richard, 99, 101
Johnny Tremain, 98
Junk reading, 52–55

K

Kaplan, Paul, 29–30
Korman, Gordon, 106
Krashen, Stephen, 53

L

Lake Villa Public Library District (Illinois), 29–30
Landsberg, Michelle, 52
Latch-key kids, 11
Lerangis, Peter, 106
Librarians
    absence in libraries of men, 8–10, 16
    and realization of gender differences, xiii
    school/public cooperation of, 47–49, 51–52
    women as (1998), 9
Libraries
    boys as disruptive in, 10, 70–71
    as feminine, 9–10
    making boys welcome at, 11–15
Light reading. *See* Junk reading
Listening skills
    booktalks and, 100–101
    reading aloud and, 96–97
Literacy, 57, 110
Lord of the Rings series, 34
Lynch, Chris, 100, 106

M

Mac Uistin, Liam, 84
Magic Tree House series, 54
Magickers, 107
Mahon, Brid, 84
"Man, the Boy, and the Donkey," 89–90
Mass media effect, 109
Medieval interests. *See* Fantasy

Mentoring, 17–18
Milne, A. A., 102
Monopoly, 66
Monsell, Mary Elise, 104
Munsinger, Lynn, 104
Myers, Laurie, 101, 103
Mystery/suspense
    booktalks and, 105–6
    programs for, 67–68
    resources for, 42
Mythology, 49

N

National Assessment of Educational Progress (NAEP), 1
Native American culture, 49
Nonfiction as boys' choice, 22–24
Nonlinear reading, 23, 26
    medieval genre and, 34

O

"Old Man and His Sons," 93
Only Way I Know, 25
Oxford County Library System (Ontario), 67

P

Parents' discussion groups, 35–36
Parlin Library Chess Program, 59–60
Paulsen, Gary, 100
Peer pressure, 44–45, 109
Phillips, Angela, xii, 4, 13, 28
Pilky, Dav, 24
Pollack, William, 36
Poof! Rabbits Everywhere, 106
Power of Reading, 53
Privacy and background checks, 16–17
Programming
    after-school, 5
    board games/role playing and, 66–67
    booktalks and, 108
    fantasy/medieval genre and, 25–37, 32–34
    involving dads and men, 19
    library promotion of reading through, xiii-xiv, 110

Programming (cont'd)
    mystery/suspense, 67–68
    planning/initiating library chess and,
        60–62
    reading aloud and, 95–96
    sports genre and, 24–25, 29–32
    summer reading programs and, 68–69

R
"Rabbit and the Rock Soup," 88
Ragucci, David, 59
Read a Ton Challenge, 69
Read Across America, 49–51
READ (Reading Education Assistance
    Dogs), 97
Reading challenges, 68–69
Reading for the Love of It, 52
Real Boys' Voices, 36
Resources
    appeal to reason approach and, 101–2
    Boy Scouts and, 55–56
    challenge approach and, 104–6
    fantasy/medieval genre and, 38–40,
        107
    guilty pleasure approach and, 102–4
    humor genre and, 41, 102–3
    mystery/suspense genre and, 42
    school/public cooperation and, 52
    science fiction genre and, 40–41
    sports genre and, 38, 106–7
Ripkin, Cal, Jr., 25
Roberts, Ken, 101
Robinson Crusoe, 101
Rockwell, Thomas, 24
Rohmann, Eric, 74
Role models, 18
Role-playing, 51, 66–67. See also Fantasy
Rowling, J. K., 32, 67
Rutan, Lynn, 30

S
Safety issues, 16–17
Saskatchewan Library Association, 67
Scheduling. See also Programming
    discussion groups with fathers and,
        35–36
    planning/initiating library chess and,
        60–62

School-library connections
    cooperation and, 47–49, 51–52
    story hours and, 48
    storytelling and, 48–49
Science fiction, 40–41
Scieszka, Jon, 24, 99, 103
Searching for Bobby Fischer, 59
Sector 7, 74
Series of Unfortunate Events, 102, 104
Seuss, Dr., 49–51
Shan, Darren, 105
"Sick Lion and the Fox," 91
Silmarillion, 34
Sis, Peter, 74
Snicket, Lemony, 102, 104
Social activities and peer pressure, 44–45
Spelling skills, 42
Sports/outdoors
    as boys' choice, 24–25
    promotion of reading and, 29–32
    resources for, 38, 106–7
Stick & Whittle, 107
"Stone Soup," 84–88
Story hours, 48
Storytelling
    "Aesop and the Bread Bag," 88–89
    "Blind Man and the Lame Man," 90
    "Cats and the Monkey," 91–92
    "Cuchulainn and the King of the Fairy
        Folk," 81–84
    exercises for, 76–79
    "Frog and the Ox," 92–93
    "Man, the Boy, and the Donkey,"
        89–90
    "Old Man and His Sons," 93
    oral, 74–75
    power of, 93–94
    reading aloud and, 95–96
    school-library cooperation for, 48–49
    "Sick Lion and the Fox," 91
    "Stone Soup," 84–88
    teaching boys in, 75–76
    visual, 74
Strategies for making boys welcome, 11–12.
        See also Programming
Summer Reading Is Killing Me, 99
Summer reading programs, 67–68, 75, 99
Surviving Brick Johnson, 101, 103

T

There's a Wocket in My Pocket, 51

This Book Really Sucks! The Science behind Gravity, Flight, Leeches, Black Holes, Tornadoes, Our Friend the Vacuum Cleaner, and Most Everything Else That Sucks, 98

Thumb in the Box, 101

Time Flies, 74

Time Warp Trio series, 54, 103

Tolkien, J. R. R., 34

"Tramp and the Old Woman," 88

Transmogrification of Roscoe Wizzle, 99, 102

Trivial Pursuit, 66

Trouble with Boys, xii, 4

U

Uncover the Mysteries, 67

Underwear!, 104

United States Chess Federation, 63

U.S. Department of Education, ix

V

Vocabulary skills, 53

Volunteers
    background checks and, 17
    non-parents as, 17–18

W

Wheeler, Mary Alice, 29

Wiesner, David, 74

Writing skills, 42, 73

MICHAEL SULLIVAN (MLS, Simmons 1999) has been a children's librarian and library director in public libraries for twelve years. He is currently director of the Weeks Public Library in Greenland, New Hampshire. An author, a traveling storyteller, and a chess instructor, Sullivan once worked at the Boston Museum of Science's overnight "Camp-In" program for children. His chess program at the Parlin Memorial Library in Everett, Massachusetts, earned an Outstanding Achievement Award in the U.S. Conference of Mayors City Livability Award competition in 2001. He is a former president of the New Hampshire Library Association and was the 1998 New Hampshire Librarian of the Year.